Staging Sex

Staging Sex lays out a comprehensive, practical solution for staging intimacy, nudity, and sexual violence.

This book takes theatre practitioners step-by-step through the best practices, tools, and techniques for crafting effective theatrical intimacy. After an overview of the challenges directors face when staging theatrical intimacy, *Staging Sex* offers practical solutions and exercises, provides a system for establishing and discussing boundaries, and suggests efficient and effective language for staging intimacy and sexual violence. It also addresses production and classroom specific concerns and provides guidance for creating a culture of consent in any company or department.

Written for directors, choreographers, movement coaches, stage managers, production managers, professional actors, and students of acting courses, *Staging Sex* is an essential tool for theatre practitioners who encounter theatrical intimacy or instructional touch, whether in rehearsal or in the classroom.

Chelsea Pace (SDC, MFA Arizona State University) is an intimacy choreographer, intimacy coordinator for film, and movement specialist. She is an Assistant Professor at the University of Maryland, Baltimore County and she choreographs and consults on best practices for staging intimacy for professional and educational theatre and film across the country. Chelsea is Co-Founder and Head Faculty of Theatrical Intimacy Education and President of the Association of Theatre Movement Educators. www.chelseapace.com and www.theatricalintimacyed.com.

Laura Rikard (AEA, SAG-AFTRA, SDC) is a director, actor, theatre educator, acting coach, and intimacy specialist. She is Co-Founder and Head Faculty of Theatrical Intimacy Education. She is an Assistant Professor of Theatre at the University of South Carolina Upstate. www.laurarikarddirector.com.

Staging Sex

Best Practices, Tools, and Techniques for Theatrical Intimacy

Chelsea Pace

With contributions from
Laura Rikard

Photography by Shealyn Jae

Models:
Hannah Kelly, Maria Marsalis, Shaquan Pearson, Barbara Pinolini, Carl Randolph, Sanjana Taskar, and Clay Vanderbeek

First published 2020
by Routledge
52 Vanderbilt Avenue, New York, NY 10017

and by Routledge
2 Park Square, Milton Park, Abingdon, Oxon, OX14 4RN

Routledge is an imprint of the Taylor & Francis Group, an informa business

© 2020 Taylor & Francis

The right of Chelsea Pace to be identified as author of this work has been asserted by her in accordance with sections 77 and 78 of the Copyright, Designs and Patents Act 1988.

All rights reserved. No part of this book may be reprinted or reproduced or utilised in any form or by any electronic, mechanical, or other means, now known or hereafter invented, including photocopying and recording, or in any information storage or retrieval system, without permission in writing from the publishers.

Trademark notice: Product or corporate names may be trademarks or registered trademarks, and are used only for identification and explanation without intent to infringe.

Library of Congress Cataloging-in-Publication Data
A catalog record for this title has been requested

ISBN: 978–1–138–59648–1 (hbk)
ISBN: 978–1–138–59649–8 (pbk)
ISBN: 978–0–429–48761–3 (ebk)

Typeset in Stone Serif
Swales & Willis, Exeter, Devon, UK

To students and their teachers. Go make it less weird.

BRIEF CONTENTS

Foreword xii
Acknowledgments xiv

Introduction 1

CHAPTER 1 *Tools and Techniques 15*

CHAPTER 2 *The Ingredients 39*

CHAPTER 3 *Staging Intimacy 73*

CHAPTER 4 *Recipes 85*

CHAPTER 5 *Production Logistics 101*

CHAPTER 6 *Staging Sex: A–Z 111*

APPENDIX *Theatrical Intimacy Education 119*

Index 121

DETAILED CONTENTS

Foreword xii

Acknowledgments xiv

Introduction 1

The Old Approaches 2

Old Approach: "Just Kiss Each Other!" 2

Old Approach: The Actors Talk It Through 3

Old Approach: The Actors Talk It Through (Over There) 3

Old Approach: Show, Don't Tell 4

Old Approach: Let the Choreographer Do It 4

Old Approach: The Sharing Circle 5

Old Approach: Chemistry Lessons 5

Getting Better at Staging Sex 6

What the Old Approaches Ignored 7

The Power in the Room: the Director 7

The Power of the Room: Human Psychology 8

How This Book Can Help: Three Big Ideas 9

Create a Culture of Consent 9

Desexualize the Process 10

Choreograph It 11

Who I Am and What This Book Is 12

CHAPTER 1   ### *Tools and Techniques 15*

Environmental Factors 15

The Boundary Tools 17

Button 17

Games for Practicing "No" and Button 19

Simon Says (with Some Twists) 19

vii

viii DETAILED CONTENTS

The Circle Game (or "Yes" with a Twist) 20

Fences 21

Gates 23

The Boundary Practice 24

Boundary Practice Modification 26

What to Say: The First Time through the Boundary Practice 27

Group Boundary Practice 29

Quick Check-Ins 30

Navigating Resistance 31

Placeholders 31

De-Roling 33

Stop Stepping In 34

Boundary Breakers 35

Joking Around 36

Additional Boundaries 36

Making Mistakes 37

CHAPTER 2   *The Ingredients 39*

Opening and Closing Distance 40

Opening and Closing Hands 41

Telling Stories 41

Directing Distance 41

Levels of Touch 42

Level 1: Skin/Powder/Touching 43

Level 2: Muscle/Paint/Moving 43

Level 3: Bone/Clay/Pulling 44

Tips for Using Levels of Touch 44

Choreographing with Levels of Touch 45

Tempo and Counts 46

Trying Counts 46

Putting It Together 47

DETAILED CONTENTS　ix

The Shapes　47

　Arcs (or Curves)　48

　Angles (or Lines)　48

　Figure Eights　48

　Putting It on Its Feet　48

Destination　49

Eye Contact　51

　Try It with a Partner　52

　Other Applications　52

Visible Power Shifts　52

　Try Visible Power Shifts　56

　Using What Ifs and Visible Power Shifts　56

Breath and Sound　57

　Short and Long　57

　Shallow and Deep　57

　High and Low　57

　Sharp　58

　Vowels and Consonants　58

　Putting Voice, Breath, and Movement Together　58

Gravity and Weight　58

　Playing with Gravity　59

　Playing with Weight　59

　Combinations with Gravity and Weight　60

Kissing　60

　Ground Rules　60

　Talk about that Kiss　61

　Opening and Closing Distance　61

　Counts　61

　Level of Touch　62

　Destination　62

x DETAILED CONTENTS

The Kiss Conversation 62

Trying It with Your Hands 62

Common Fixes for Bad Kisses 63

Alternatives to Kisses 64

Putting the Ingredients to Work 65

Choreographing 65

Tweaking 66

Documenting 67

Writing Recipes 67

Notating and Coaching Choreography 68

Actor Documentation 70

Production Documentation 70

Practicing with an Open Scene 70

CHAPTER 3   *Staging Intimacy 73*

Who is in the Room 73

Vulnerability 73

Practicing Vulnerability 74

Partner Up 75

Put It in Motion 75

Introduce Touch 77

Moving Together 78

Staging Sexual Violence 80

De-Roling in Sexual Violence 82

Staging Nudity 82

Have a Backup Plan 83

Additional Thoughts 84

CHAPTER 4   *Recipes 85*

Embrace 85

Variations 87

Kiss 87

Variations 88

DETAILED CONTENTS   **xi**

Oral Sex   89

Masturbation and/or Digital Stimulation   91

Penetrative Sex   93

Feeling and Touching   95

Teasing   96

Removing Clothes   97

Intimacy with Lots of Text   98

Stylization   98

CHAPTER 5   *Production Logistics   101*

Company and Department Policies   101

Chain of Communication   101

Casting   102

Audition Disclosure Form   102

Placeholders in Auditions   104

Recasting and Reimagining   104

Rehearsal Schedules   105

Intimacy Calls   105

Intimacy Choreographers   105

Staffing the Production   106

Considerations for Designers and Technicians   107

Front of House Staff and Ushers   108

Content Warnings   108

Boundaries with the Audience   109

Talkbacks   109

Post-Show Reviews   109

CHAPTER 6   *Staging Sex: A–Z   111*

Strategies for Actors   114

Strategies for Teachers   115

The Cheat Sheet   116

APPENDIX   *Theatrical Intimacy Education   119*

Index   121

FOREWORD

This book should be required reading for any theatre maker who stages scenes involving intimacy, nudity, or sexual violence. The theatre is a magical space, a liminal realm where abstract ideas about aesthetics, narrative, societal issues, and human motivation meet concrete concerns of time, space, and action to produce a potentially transcendent artistic experience. But the theatre is also a workplace, where the safety and ethical treatment of our co-workers should be of paramount concern. It's a workplace, moreover, with requirements that often fall outside the scope of the social norms and formal guidelines that govern the behavior of office, factory, education, and service sector employees. Actors routinely say and do things in the course of their jobs that would be unacceptable in other contexts, from shouting obscenities to breaking into song. Audiences have been conditioned, by well-established conventions, to recognize the action occurring on stage as "not real" – when Othello (spoiler alert) smothers Desdemona with a pillow, we don't rush forward to intervene. Yet anyone who has spent time in a rehearsal room knows that what appears to be "make believe" for an audience may be all too real for a performer.

This uncomfortable reality becomes most apparent when dealing with the physical body. When a character disrobes, it is the actor's body that is exposed. When two characters kiss, it is the actors' lips meeting. And when characters simulate sexual activity, it is the actors who may find themselves a little too close to their co-worker's "naughty bits" with disturbing regularity. The oft-repeated disclaimer "it's just a play" flies in the face of a wealth of experience that convinces us otherwise.

Staging Sex provides techniques for staging intimate or sexualized scenes in ways that help actors and directors navigate this space between the representational and the real. For directors, if you just want your make-out scene to look better, this book will help you do that. It's filled with practical tips about whose nose goes where and how to use field-tested, repeatable technique instead of unpredictable "chemistry" to get the scene where you want it to go, and to keep it there night after night.

But the greater contribution of *Staging Sex* lies in its simple-but-effective reorientation of rehearsal practice to put affirmative consent and actor safety front and center. No more pressuring an actor to the point of tears (or worse) "for the good of the show." No more assuming that everything's fine because an actor hasn't complained. No more requiring an actor to have awkward, cringe-inducing personal conversations with their scene partner or their director.

For those of us making theatre in educational contexts, where our rehearsal room is not just a workplace but a classroom, this consent-based approach is especially critical. The old approach of "if you can't handle it, maybe you shouldn't be a theatre major" is simply unacceptable for a program committed to creating and maintaining an equitable, diverse, and inclusive environment for all students.

Those in leadership roles – department chairs and artistic directors – will find *Staging Sex* especially valuable. The book's simple, workable strategies for managing power dynamics in a studio context will significantly reduce the number of office visits from distraught performers, while its readily-adaptable set of best practices on issues such as production photography and what information to include in casting calls can jump start overdue conversations about policies and procedures.

In short, this book should be required reading for any theatre maker – full stop.

Henry Bial
Chair, Department of Theatre and Dance, University of Kansas
Past President, Association for Theatre in Higher Education
Lawrence, Kansas 2019

ACKNOWLEDGMENTS

To every actor, director, teacher, choreographer, stage manager, and maker that I have had the privilege of sharing a rehearsal room with, thank you from the very bottom of my heart. Whether we worked together for a short time or for years, you have made this research possible and I am forever grateful.

Thanks to all of my mentors, friends, teachers, and colleagues. There are far too many people deserving thanks to name them all, but everything would have been far more daunting without the kindness and generosity of Annette Thornton, Henry Bial, Samantha Riedel, and Jason Davids Scott. Thanks also to the Association of Theatre Movement Educators and my wonderful colleagues at The University of Maryland Baltimore County.

To all of my collaborators at Theatrical Intimacy Education, thank you for believing in this work and for your investment in helping it grow.

Laura Rikard, thank you for being the best co-founder, co-teacher, and co-researcher anyone could ever ask for. I can't wait to see what we do next. Maisie and Ellie, thank you for letting me borrow your mom. She's amazing and so are you.

Thanks to Robin Abrahams for her keen edits. Without you this book would have made much less sense.

And to the team at Routledge, Lucia Accorsi and Stacey Walker — thank you for your support and the deadlines that made this thing real.

Thank you to my family. I know my specialty is weird, but you were proud of me anyway, even when you needed to explain what your daughter/sister/granddaughter did for a living to your friends. Thank you for opening the door to the education that set me on the path to pursue this dream.

And finally, to my Karl. Thank you for your love and support. Thank you for cheering me on and reminding me that this was possible. Thank you for keeping our many, many animals happy and fed while I was rehearsing, traveling, and writing. Thank you for doing our laundry. Thank you for being my teammate. I love you. You're my favorite. You know the rest.

Introduction

Boundaries are complicated.

Theatrical Intimacy Education[1] has buttons that say "Ask me about my Boundaries," and people take handfuls at workshops. Because most people spend a fair amount of mental energy negotiating boundaries, their own and everyone else's, on matters ranging from parking spaces to pronouns.

And that's just everyday life. Now imagine the rehearsal room. There are all the normal social boundaries that need to be negotiated among a group of people from different backgrounds, of different ages and genders and personal histories, who are sharing space and working together. On top of that, there are the professional roles that each person has taken on —performer, director, stage manager, dresser—each with its own bounded set of tasks and sphere of authority. And on top of that, there is that essential, critical boundary between the *truth* of the stage story the team is creating and the *reality* of the people in the room.

Why do so many boundaries get crossed between actors staging intimacy? Because actors kiss. Actually kiss. The contact is real. They physically put their bodies on other people's bodies and share contact that has no obvious separation from reality. Theatre artists haven't had an established technique to rely on that tells us that this is a construction, and choreography, and a craft. Because the only direction the director can give is that it needs to be more passionate and sensual. And it starts to seem like it actually is passionate and sensual. And not just blocking and not just characters. And someone's hand is up an actor's shirt and it's unclear if it is their scene partner or a character. And is it truth or reality guiding the hand on their ribcage?

Given the overlapping, intersecting, idiosyncratic, and evolving boundaries in any theatrical endeavor, it is no wonder that staging intimacy is especially charged for both actors and directors. And yet, there has been no codified system or vocabulary developed either to make the process less fraught, or to give intimacy choreography the same status as other forms of movement storytelling. This book is an attempt to fill that gap. This is a comprehensive technique, a system of tools, best practices, and vocabulary, to help you stage intimacy, nudity, and sexual violence.

THE OLD APPROACHES

Directors wouldn't ever tell two actors to "just punch each other," so how did "just kiss each other" become a part of our vernacular in the rehearsal room? It's a complicated question, but the simple answer is that historically, it has worked. For ages and eons, actors kissed when someone told them to.

So, while there hasn't been a complete system for staging intimacy, there have been approaches and techniques to make the inevitably awkward at least somewhat easier. The path to ethical, efficient, and effective theatrical intimacy is littered with good intentions. Many of the approaches people take have been created out of a genuine desire to be careful and considerate—sometimes, unfortunately, to the point of making a lot of things a lot more complicated, and maybe even worse.

Let's look at some of the most common approaches for staging intimacy, why directors and choreographers have tried them, and why they don't work.

Old Approach: "Just Kiss Each Other!"

When a director wants the actors to kiss, tell them to just kiss each other. If the director is staging intercourse, tell them what position to get into so they aren't just guessing and the sightlines work. Keep it simple!

- Why we try it

This seems like the most obvious, quickest, least awkward approach for many directors. And if the actors weren't okay with it, they would speak up. Right?

- Why it doesn't work

Maybe they won't speak up. The obvious issue here is the power dynamics in the rehearsal room. More on this later, but in short, actors are reticent to say no. It's built into their training to say yes.

The other problem is that this approach, which isn't your best bet, relies on the actors and director having the same image of the intimacy. If someone tells two actors to make out on the couch, and they do something that's awkward, or not what the director wanted, what can be done about it? Ask them to make out on the couch ... better? If the playwright has written a moment of oral sex, and the actors have *absolutely no idea* what oral sex looks like (or they are mortified that you might learn what they *think* it looks like) (or they only know about how oral sex looks in pornography) then the production is out of luck and stuck relying on one of the other Old Approaches.

Also, it's super awkward for the actors to have their director (or professor) suggesting sex positions to them.

Old Approach: The Actors Talk It Through

Ask the actors what they think the characters would do with each other and then have them try it.

- Why we try it

They are playing the roles, so the actors have the best insight here. Also, actors won't suggest anything they aren't okay with.

- Why it doesn't work

Actors will indeed suggest things they're uncomfortable with if they believe it's what the director wants.

This approach also narrows the emotional distance between actor and character. If one scene partner says they think their character wants to grope the other character, the other scene partner might be left wondering if their scene partner just wants to feel them up. That can open the door to some messy feelings down the road.

Also, the actor's ideas might not work. They might not have any real world experience, or a different experience than their character, and they might suggest an inappropriate choice. Then you are left having to explain to actors why what they want to try is an inappropriate, or boring, or super weird intimate choice. An approach that avoids awkward conversations would be best.

Old Approach: The Actors Talk It Through (Over There)

Send the actors to another room to block the intimacy on their own, maybe with an assistant stage manager to keep time and supervise.

- Why we try it

This is an attempt to allow the actors some freedom, but allows them the benefit of privacy while they experiment. It also removes the director from awkward conversations.

- Why it doesn't work

Actors are absolutely terrified of displeasing directors. They know that they need to say "yes, and", to be bold, to take risks, to make big choices. That works great in a monologue or even when staging a scene, but when actors are put in the pressure cooker of coming up with something on their own (with no skill set to fall back on other than that they should "take risks") they often stage things that make one, both, or all of the actors involved uncomfortable.

Beyond that, this isn't a great working environment for actors (not to mention the hapless assistant stage manager). If a director or choreographer isn't involved in the process, it's impossible to know how the actors came up with it (was it a consensual, comfortable process?) or how they feel about it (other than the slightly panicked/overly confident "fine" they will give you when you ask how it went).

And as with the earlier approaches, it will also be impossible to tweak it further because you aren't all working from the same set of vocabulary. A director might have to fall back on "more seductive" or "less tentative" to get what they're looking for.

Old Approach: Show, Don't Tell

Get up and show the actors what you want them to do. Work with an assistant, a cast member, or by yourself, if you're flexible enough, to demonstrate how you want things to look.

- Why we try it

If you don't have the vocabulary, this is the fastest way to show actors exactly what it is you're looking for. You check with the assistant or the actors to make sure they don't mind, and you step in to demonstrate. In dance and stage combat, this is standard practice, it's efficient, and it works.

- Why it doesn't work (for intimacy)

Even though this is a common practice in other areas of theatre, intimate scenes require a little more space between the director and the actors. There's an entire chapter about boundaries later in the book, and (spoilers) this approach crosses almost all of them.

Additionally, you might demonstrate things that the actors aren't physically able to do. And now they can picture you doing them.

Old Approach: Let the Choreographer Do It

Send in the pros.

- Why we try it

There's already a dance or fight choreographer on your team, or on your faculty, or in the cast, or within shouting distance. They are good at teaching people how to move together to tell a story and they choreograph tricky stuff all of the time. Let specialists do specialist things.

- Why it doesn't work

Dance and fight choreographers have training that does not automatically translate to an intimacy setting. Both dance and fight choreography rely extensively on demonstration from the instructor—which can be absolutely fine when demonstrating a lift or a partnered fall, but crosses a boundary for intimacy. Fight choreographers are used to saying "punch" when they mean "fake punch," so it's easy to understand why they say things like "let's do the rape scene" when they mean, "let's work on the scene where we tell the story of an assault."

Fight choreographers often rely on an actor to imagine specific injuries and real danger to tell the story of the hits and misses. Asking an actor to imagine the realities of sexual violence, or even consensual intimacy, is a psychological exercise that can be emotionally damaging and triggering.

Old Approach: The Sharing Circle

Take the time to understand everyone's relationship to intimacy and the material in the scene so you can approach the material carefully.

- Why we try it

You're considerate, thoughtful, and concerned that the material might be triggering (or just uncomfortable) for the actors. You want them to understand that you recognize that this is difficult and it's important to you that you give them space to voice their concerns. This will also help the actors personalize the intimate moments.

- Why it doesn't work

While imagining that an action or event or prop for a character is something from the actor's lived experience might be a good idea, actors personalizing the intimate or violent events of the play for themselves can create unsafe situations. Making the events of a play personal for the actor means that the world of the play and reality are now in overlapping bubbles. That overlap can encourage confusion, showmance, tech week breakdowns, real world break ups, and all around messy choreography.

This sets you up for a bad situation if actors reveal trauma that you (and the rest of the ensemble) aren't equipped to handle. Even the most emotionally intelligent, mental health first-aid certified director isn't a therapist, and rehearsal isn't therapy. An actor reliving their personal trauma on stage every night isn't going to make your play better and it has the potential to damage the actor's emotional well-being.

Old Approach: Chemistry Lessons

Have the actors do a series of exercises and improvisations to help them feel the energy between them. Guide them to observe how it feels to be touched by their partner. Tell them to imagine their partner's body and think about how it moves. Get them to fall a little bit in love.

- Why we try it

If the actors were actually into each other, this scene would be so much better. It would probably block itself and you wouldn't have to worry about anyone's boundaries getting crossed. They wouldn't be so awkward and the play would be better.

- Why it doesn't work

Relying on actor emotions is an unreliable and unstable way of working. Passion fades. Choreography is forever. They might not like each other in six weeks. Or they might like each other more than is helpful or useful. Relying on "chemistry" is the express train to Showmanceville.

This approach also creates an environment where reality and the truth of the play are equated. If you are asking them to develop real feelings towards each other, they will have a much harder time shaking off the scene when it's over. And if the intimacy in the play is meant to be traumatic or violent, this approach signals to the actors that you want them feeling and living that trauma and betrayal every night.

GETTING BETTER AT STAGING SEX

All of the previous approaches to staging intimacy fell short in at least one of two major areas: getting full and informed consent from the actors, and/or creating consistent ways to communicate the artistic demands of the scene.

There are three problems with current practices around staging intimacy:

1. The dynamics of the rehearsal room make consent tricky and leaves the door open to abuses of power.

2. Even in the absence of abuse or wrongdoing, the nature of theatrical intimacy makes actors psychologically, physically, and emotionally vulnerable, and good intentions on the part of their directors and scene partners are not sufficient to protect them. People who work with volatile substances— like explosives, or human neurotransmitters and hormones—need more than mutual respect to keep things from blowing up. They need ultra-clear communication and a protocol.

3. Intimate moments onstage are part of the story and deserve the same attention to detail and careful crafting as any other moment of theatrical storytelling. We need better tools to tell those stories.

Unfortunately, identifying shortcomings (while an honored theatrical tradition) no more creates a system than sharing horror stories (also an honored theatrical tradition) creates a solution.

This book is a path towards a comprehensive solution for staging intimacy, nudity, and sexual violence designed in response to the needs of directors, actors, stage managers, choreographers, and audience members.

- We need to get consent from *everyone* involved in the process every step of the way.

- We need to establish and normalize clear boundaries for *everyone*.

INTRODUCTION **7**

- We need to treat theatrical intimacy as choreography and choreograph it in a way that is directable, efficient, and doesn't fall apart in front of an *audience*.

- We need to stop putting the burden of staging the scenes on the shoulders of *actors*.

- We need to give our *stage managers* something to write down better than "just kiss each other."

Staging intimacy, nudity, and sexual violence is tricky because boundaries—physical, professional, emotional—can so easily get crossed. But we can do better.

WHAT THE OLD APPROACHES IGNORED

For decades, "just kiss each other" seemed to work. Actors kissed! It seemed fine!

But the old approaches ignored the power *in* the rehearsal room, and the power *of* the rehearsal room. They were based on the assumption that good intentions were all that were necessary to create a good experience for the cast (and ultimately the audience). This assumption is incorrect. Let's examine why.

The Power in the Room: the Director

No matter how egalitarian, consensus-based, and all-around awesome and approachable you may be, you are still the director, the authority in the room. When you are the one in charge, the cast has been conditioned into certain attitudes through years of training to see you and your requests in a certain way.

(Please note: Not all projects are the same, and age, race, gender, disability, experience, education, union status, who's new in town and who has an established network, who has a trust fund and who supports themselves, also influence the power dynamics in the room. The particulars of this section, however, deal with actors' conditioning and some basic principles of psychology.)

As the director you may not feel powerful—you probably feel stressed, underpaid, underslept, overjoyed, frustrated, elated, all in different measures. But those feelings don't undermine your power. Neither does a good intimacy practice. This system is not about empowering actors at the expense of directors, but rather actors and directors alike gaining a vocabulary to meet the demands of the art they are creating together.

Actors are trained to say yes. Acting school is an exercise in saying yes to everything. They have been trained from day one that the first rule is "yes, and," and there is a standard that actors are expected to meet and that they are, in all ways, "easy to work with." The message they internalize is that they can't ruffle any feathers, ask any hard questions, or say no. They believe saying no, or even questioning a direction, might make them "hard to work with." The "Easy to Work With Myth" is pervasive. By sending the message that an actor is a person that says "yes," and takes risks, it comes through loud and clear that a person looking to protect themselves and says no isn't cut out to be an actor.

When an actor doesn't know how a director will feel about them establishing clear boundaries, with their reputation potentially on the line, they will say yes, knowing that "yes, and" is the safest choice. Actors are taught that their reputations are as valuable, or more valuable, than their boundaries.

Actors are professionally vulnerable. Actors are taught, either through formal training or observation of the industry, that they are replaceable. Directors can fire actors on the spot. They can keep them from getting future work. Actors learn they are at the bottom early on in their training. They say yes for the sake of being "easy to work with" in an attempt to keep their jobs and be hired again. Performers internalize the message that saying yes is staying employed. A performer fearing that a "hard to work with" label might make them say "okay" to being touched in a way that makes them uncomfortable. They might agree to nudity that wasn't in their contract. They might go home in tears, frustrated that the skewed power dynamic of a performer and director/producer left them feeling powerless.

The Power *of* the Room: Human Psychology

Even if the rehearsal room were a completely flat hierarchy—an improv group with a new leader chosen randomly at each meeting, say—the people in it would *still* have a hard time saying "no," simply because of the power of group dynamics. Directors should be aware of three psychological phenomena:

People conform. Humans are mutually dependent and learn by imitation, and one of the side effects of that is a very strong tendency to conform. People will deny simple logic and the evidence of their own senses in order to fit in with a group—getting them to ignore their own comfort levels is easy. No one wants to be the one to redirect the flow or change the mood of a room. Being the first one to say "no" is the hardest.

At its extreme, conformity can lead to what management experts call the "Abilene Paradox," when a group agrees on a course of action that few, if any of them, actually want to undertake because one person introduced the idea, another supports it to be polite, and then everyone thinks everyone *else* thinks it's a great idea.

People need protocol. Respect and courtesy are important to everyone, but the behavior language used to express them differs from culture to culture. Do you take off your hat to pray or put it on? Is it more polite to accept or decline food that is offered to you? When are gifts appropriate? Without a shared behavioral language, it is difficult to interpret other people's behavior or feel confident that your own will be interpreted correctly.

This is why having explicit protocol or team culture is important when dealing with a diverse team and/or complicated interpersonal relationships—both of which conditions apply in just about any rehearsal room. We have these protocols around many areas of theatre, but historically not when staging intimacy, where it's arguably the most needed.

Heightened states affect cognition. People's brains work differently when they are in a state of high arousal—stressed, adrenalized, *on*, like actors once rehearsal starts to get real. The unconscious mind looks for a good primitive reason for that heightened state and may decide it's due to an attractive scene partner, not stage fright. Boundary-setting and other higher-order social skills may tend to decline, unless those skills are practiced in a heightened state.

HOW THIS BOOK CAN HELP: THREE BIG IDEAS

The goal is that in every rehearsal room, someone should have access to, and actually use, a system for staging intimacy, nudity, and sexual violence. The plan for making that happen is to have that person be you. Not every organization or production can, or necessarily needs to, hire an intimacy choreographer. If they can, great, but the goal is to continue to make the people already in the room be better at being in the room. The target audience for this book is directors, choreographers, and theatre teachers. These are the people who are most powerful and most present in the rehearsal room.

Actors, stage managers, and students: the best practices in this book are a starting point for you to have a conversation with the people in power in your rehearsal rooms about how things can be better. Every technique that I outline in this book is a tool that you can take into a scene study, into rehearsal, into your career with you.

This book is particularly important for college and high school teachers because student actors are particularly vulnerable—their directors assign not only roles but grades and recommendation letters. By training emerging artists in ethical, efficient, and decidedly desexualized practices, we can work to eliminate a culture of ineffective, traumatizing staged intimacy.

Three main guide this book. If you get overwhelmed, come back here.

1. Create a Culture of Consent

Directors like to think that they don't pressure actors to do things that they don't want to do. They may point to safeguards in their rehearsal rooms, union protections, their own affable personalities and approachability. You can be the most approachable, seemingly least threatening director in the world, but at the end of the day, you hold the power in the situation. You can't give it away by being approachable.

And you shouldn't. Because of the power *of* the room, you need to be the power *in* the room. If you don't break the tendency toward conformity, who will? If you don't provide techniques to reinforce the boundary between the actor and the role, who will? It's up to you to learn how to use your power. Bring best practices in the room. Model good behavior.

For example, if the ensemble decides that everyone gives everyone else back-rubs, offer a practice for the actors to get consent from each other, but don't participate. If you are tempted to join in, imagine the creepiest director you have ever worked with jumping into that massage train. No, you aren't them, but if you do it, it normalizes directors crossing professional boundaries. Don't do anything your creepiest colleague shouldn't. Because if you do, your creepiest colleague might think it's okay. Look out for the actors by modeling good behavior, even if you think you can get away with less. Have better boundaries than you think you need.

No ethical director wants to take advantage of the actor-director power dynamic. Consent requires an enthusiastic, uncoerced "yes" from all parties involved, so an "I guess so, sure," out of obligation hardly qualifies. When a conscientious director becomes aware of this power dynamic, they try to close that gap by empowering the actor to establish boundaries, making an effort to check in, or calling in a pro. That director works hard to make sure the actor is comfortable with whatever tools they have at their disposal.

To actually get consent in the rehearsal room, there has to be space, real space, for the actor to say "no." It's not enough to tell actors that they can say "no." If your whole training life has conditioned you to say yes, saying "no" breaks the rules. Even asking for a moment to decide can feel like being difficult. Even when you ask them what they want, actors feel the pressure to be easy.

It's not enough to tell actors that they can say "no." **We need to normalize "no,"** and we do that by establishing an expectation, with words and with our actions, that everyone will have boundaries and those boundaries will be respected. I tell actors all the time that there is no boundary that will get in the way of my ability to tell a story. And I mean it.

This system ensures that we are starting off on the right foot by building consent into every step of the process. We have a consent-based boundary establishment, consent-based choreography, and consent-focused methods. We normalize asking questions and setting boundaries so that when we get a yes, they mean it.

2. Desexualize the Process

Staging sex doesn't need to be sexy—it shouldn't be, any more than staging violence should be scary. Keep any illusion of actual sexiness out of the process with clear boundaries, clear choreography, and desexualized language.

Desexualized language describes the physical pieces of the movement and skips over the cultural or social context the movement is usually given. For example, in a handshake, there is contact between the palms, medium pressure with the fingertips on the back of your partner's hand, synchronized motion up and down, and a release. Working this way for a handshake might seem silly, but it gives the director room to craft and shape the handshake. Slow it down, speed it up, increase pressure, be out of sync.

All of those tiny cues tell us about character and circumstance without the director needing to say, "be tentative," "be passionate," "be aggressive," or "make it awkward." That same breakdown makes intimacy directable and keeps directors from relying on vague psychological cues, like "be more passionate" or "struggle more". When you use desexualized language to describe intimacy, you avoid describing sex acts to actors, but you gain an ability to direct the movement as specifically as you might like.

Describe everything in desexualized language. Don't call the scene with intimacy in it "the sex scene." Call it Act II scene ii, or the "coffee shop scene."

When we desexualize the language, we never *grope* our scene partners. That would be highly unprofessional and rude. We instead *find muscle- and bone-level contact with the areas of our partner's bodies that they have given us permission to work with today*. We don't *hump* our partners. We *open and close the distance between our pelvises*. We don't *struggle to get away*, we *apply bone level contact, short sharp breath, open distance, and avoid eye contact while they try and close distance and seek eye contact*. Equally important to choreographing with desexualized language is to keep a desexualized rehearsal space. Avoid making sexual comments in rehearsal and encourage everyone to use the desexualized language of the choreography, rather than realistic sexual language. Euphemisms like "getting it on" or "horny" can create discomfort in the room. Don't worry if you slip up, it's about creating a culture, not being 100% perfect.

Every intimate scene can be broken down, desexualized, and directed with this system. When movement is described in concrete, desexualized terms, it can be easily written down, leaving the actors with a recipe that they can follow into tech week and beyond.

3. Choreograph It

Choreography is your insurance policy against all sorts of weirdness.

If you want a passionate kiss, the first day you say "just passionately kiss each other" the actors might do exactly what you want them to do. They might feel great about it and do it consistently for the duration of the run and it never gets weird and they never change it. Perfection. That's almost never how it goes. Or at least it's not the whole story.

What if they do exactly what you want them to do the first time and then never again? What if they get the giggles every time they go in for it after that? How do you get the passionate magic back? It's never as good again and you are left googling synonyms for passionate.

What if they do it weird the first time? You say passionate kiss, and you get an awkward face smashing, writhing mess that you can't do anything about. What can you say to them? Kiss better? Kiss less weirdly? If you can't shape it, there is no guarantee that the intimacy will tell the story you are trying to tell.

What if you say kiss passionately, it goes perfectly all the way through opening night? It all seems fine, but by closing, one of the actors is in tears because their partner keeps crossing the line, adding moves, getting handsy, night after night, and your stage manager has no idea how to get them back on track?

Without choreography, boundaries getting crossed left and right, things changing depending on actor whims and moods is the norm. And when theatrical intimacy is loosely set, it's not only a boundary nightmare, it's undirectable. That incredible kiss they just found? It's gone if you don't know how to go back and get it and then set it.

Intimacy needs to be choreographed. And if you treat intimacy as choreography, you can tell exactly the story you want to tell without needing to rely on the ingenuity and sexual experience of your actors.

The process for choreographing it can range widely, from a collaborative, exploratory approach to the director having a crystal clear concept or idea going in. And just like how spins become pirouettes when choreographing a dance, choreographing intimacy needs its own vocabulary. It's important that we assign movements vocabulary because without language, it becomes very difficult to record the choreography.

Passion fades. Choreography is forever. I want to help directors and choreographers realize on stage what they can see in their heads, so if you are directing *Romeo and Juliet*, and you knew what you want it to look like, you are able to put the scene together yourself in a way that made everyone feel great about it.

Long story short: If you want it to be repeatable, choreograph it. If you want it to tell a consistent story, choreograph it. If you want to help your stage manager run the show, choreograph it. If you want happy actors, choreograph it.

WHO I AM AND WHAT THIS BOOK IS

First and foremost, I am a woman who wore Good Underwear to rehearsal every day for six weeks because my director never told me when Underwear Rehearsal would be. There was no standard protocol for communicating this sort of thing to actors at the time. I didn't feel traumatized or anxious or exploited or anything like that. I loved working with the director, and I was having a marvelous time, except for how much time I spent doing laundry. It got me thinking there had to be a better way.

In my training, no one taught me how to be in intimacy on stage. Theatrical intimacy has been left completely out of the curriculum. That led to an awful lot of worry, confusion, and general boundary fuzziness. If the stage direction says kiss, should I go ahead and kiss my scene partner? Are they going to kiss me? That's good, right? If I ask about the kiss, am I overeager, or does that mean I'm so naive that I don't know that you just kiss each other? I wanted to save other theatre artists the awkwardness and confusion I experienced.

I have made or witnessed many of the mistakes I am going to ask you not to make. It's not because I didn't care about the safety or boundaries of actors I was working with. It is because, like many directors and choreographers, I didn't have a comprehensive system for staging intimacy, nudity, and sexual violence when I got started and things slipped through the cracks. I could not have written this without every actor and director with whom I have shared a rehearsal room. I learned from all of their examples, good and bad. I saw what mistakes looked like from people with good intentions and what abuse looked like from people with bad ones.

I developed this system to be fast, easy, and accessible. Rehearsal time is a precious commodity and the speedy-if-unreliable "just kiss each other!" held the time to beat. This system—tested extensively in professional and academic rehearsal studios, on set, and in classrooms across the country—can be learned quickly and doesn't take a lot of in-rehearsal time.

This book is my method for staging intimacy. Not all of it is for everyone, and that's fine. Borrow in whole or in part the bits that make sense to you. Think of it as a cookbook. As with a cookbook, you can make things as simple, or as complicated and customized as you like. Only you are responsible for what you do with it. Please take the time to understand the "why" of a section before you bring it into your rehearsal room, but then bring it into the rehearsal room and make it yours. This is a toolkit designed to supplement and work with your own.

This system was developed for live theatre and it is designed to be the most-cautious, considerate, and thoughtful version of a system for staging theatrical intimacy. A system was designed to work for students in academia, some of the most vulnerable people in the industry, works beautifully for experienced professionals.

The Ingredients will give you all of the tools you need to create beautiful choreography. This book is not a choreography lesson, but a translation manual with a whole bunch of commonly used phrases. The Recipes and Ingredients you will find in this book are designed to make intimacy easier to choreograph. They give you specific language that describes movements, not sex acts. That specificity means that every move is infinitely tweakable.

If you get overwhelmed: Get consent, desexualize it, and choreograph it. Even a little bit better is better. You got this. Let's jump in.

---

[1] For more about Theatrical Intimacy Education, see Appendix.

CHAPTER 1

Tools and Techniques

ENVIRONMENTAL FACTORS

For all of the tools and techniques to work effectively, a few rehearsal environment tweaks may be needed to set the tone for the process. Using the following phrases can contribute to a positive, consent-based working environment:

- **Say, "Your boundaries are perfect exactly where they are."**

This helps normalize boundary setting. Performers have long been told that their boundaries are a hindrance, so this seemingly obvious statement goes a long way to make it clear that the actors have a right to their boundaries. This statement helps relieve a lot of actors' worry about what they might be asked to do, and also reminds everyone to not take anyone else's boundaries personally.

- **Say, "It's ok if your boundaries change. Check in on boundaries with your partner."**

Circumstances and context change the way touch is received. Only the boundary-holder can negotiate their boundaries, not anyone else. Directors unknowingly ask performers to ignore or change their boundaries all the time. Scene partners can be even worse offenders. Reminding everyone who controls the boundaries and enforcing that performer boundaries are the law of the rehearsal-land continues to establish performer autonomy.

When introducing the idea of a check-in, give examples of how checking-in can be a neutral, or even positive thing. Don't assume the actors will casually let you know if things change. Checking in on boundaries, or someone's comfort level, can be complicated if the process isn't formalized. Actively normalizing boundary check-ins allows for performers to take responsibility for maintaining and updating their boundaries as the process progresses.

- **Ask "May I touch you?" and "Would you like a hug?"**

There is an assumption that all theatre people are touchy and interested in hugs. Start asking in rehearsal and in life.

15

- **Ask "Does that work for you?" "What are your thoughts on that?" or "How do you feel about that?"**

In school, you may have learned that asking open questions was the key to getting interesting answers. An open question is one that doesn't have an implied, or expected answer. "Is that ok?" sets an expectation that the answer is "yes, that's ok." But the question, "How does that work for you?" doesn't have a built-in answer. The answerer might realize they aren't sure how something works for them. They take an extra second to orient themselves to your question and to consult their boundaries before they answer. That little bit of extra flexibility takes unintentional pressure off of the performer to say what they think you want to hear.

Open questions aren't just for directors. In rehearsal, open questions between actors are key to understanding clear boundaries and to developing interesting choreography that works for everyone. If a scene partner says, "I'll hug you at the end of my line," there isn't a lot of room for the other partner to consider their boundaries around a hug. "What do you think about a hug at the end of the line?" still suggests a hug, but leaves room for a counterproposal. Rather than having to reject the suggestion outright to preserve boundaries, or say "yes" to avoid rocking the boat, the actor can take a beat, consult their boundaries, and make a suggestion.

Instead of "can I touch your shoulder?" try "how would you feel about me touching your shoulder at this moment?" Replace "you okay with that?" with "what do you think?" Rather than "grab his face," ask "what do you think comes next?"

Open questions create opportunities for everyone to consider what is being asked of them and to make suggestions that work for their boundaries.

- **Say: "Let's get you some support."**

Rehearsal processes can be intense. Particularly if you are working with potentially triggering material, actors may need support beyond what the production can, or should, provide. If a member of the production is in crisis, don't tell them to "use it" in the scene and resist any urge to play therapist. It can be traumatizing to the person in crisis, traumatizing to the other people in the room, and it crosses professional boundaries when unqualified people try and take responsibility for the mental health of others.

If things get emotional in rehearsal, remember that while theatre may be therapeutic, it's not therapy. Maintaining good boundaries, supporting good technique, and enlisting the appropriate resources are all you can to do to take care of your ensemble mentally and emotionally in rehearsal. Assemble a resource page and include it in the handouts at the first rehearsal. Include hot line and resource center numbers. Check for community centers that might provide counselling at low or no cost. If you are on a campus, add information about university counselling services. Have a crisis plan and know how to reach professionals.

Taking on an emotional support role as a director blurs the line for the ensemble about your role in the process. If a member of the ensemble needs emotional support, be compassionate and refer them to a professional.

THE BOUNDARY TOOLS

There are three tools for establishing boundaries in rehearsal:

- Button

- Fences

- Gates

Those tools come together in an exercise called The Boundary Practice. The Boundary Practice is an exercise designed to address the complex problems of unclear expectations and general awkwardness around negotiating consensual touch. Many directors have developed versions of some of these tools to begin to address the complexities of establishing boundaries, but it is this comprehensive combination of tools makes The Boundary Practice effective.

Please note: The Boundary Practice has two major components: a physical exercise and a verbal reinforcement. It is critical that the physical exercise precedes the verbal. Verbal boundary establishment may seem quicker, but when used alone it leaves more room for common scripts and expectations to take hold. "You can touch me anywhere," is something an "easy to work with" actor might say, or feel pressured to say. "You can touch me anywhere," pressures their partner to say, "yeah, me too." "Is that ok?" is an often uttered phrase by conscientious educators and respectful partners, but it has an implied, or expected answer: "yes." Ask as room of people where their upper thigh begins and you will get as many answers as there are people in the room. The issue with verbal boundaries is that they are more susceptible to generalization and social pressure than physically established ones.

To understand the complete Boundary Practice, let's first look at the individual tools.

BUTTON

The Button is a word that indicates that the action needs to pause for a moment. Pauses might be to ask a question, clear something up, shake something out, or even to avoid sneezing into someone's face. Calling "hold" or "stop" or even "wait" can feel like too much of a fuss if someone just needs a moment.

Introduce The Button to your whole ensemble early and remind them of it often, preferably before any staging begins. Giving them space to pause and ask questions gives them more opportunities to say "yes."

18 TOOLS AND TECHNIQUES

Choosing a Button Word

The Button word should be a word that is easy for the ensemble to remember. It can be fun to let each cast or class choose a Button, but that can lead actors to fumbling to remember which word is the right word in a heightened moment. "Button" is easy to remember (it's the "Pause Button") and it's easy to say.

If you decide to use a different word, there are two rules when choosing a Button word:

1. The Button word exists outside of the world of the play. It shouldn't appear in the script and should be a word unlikely to come up in rehearsal. Even if the characters never say "computer," if there is a computer on the set, find a word other than "computer" to be your Button.
2. The Button word needs to be neutral. That means:

   a. The Button can't have another meaning like "fire" or "help"
   b. The Button isn't a word that substitutes "stop" in other contexts. That defeats the purpose of making it easier to say. Stay away from "pause" and "wait."

Effective Button words include:

- Button
- Camp
- Racecar
- Canada
- Tofu
- Rodeo
- Polar Bear
- California
- Tangerine

The Button is an effective tool that helps the process along on several fronts. The first is that it keeps the actors from becoming self-indulgent. Rather than spending precious time explaining why they need a break, an actor can say the Button, shake it out, and get back to work. The second is that it helps with boundary maintenance. Say the Button, ask your partner for permission or clarification, and continue right where you left off. Button is calling line on boundaries. Third, the Button helps prevent actors from emotionally hijacking a rehearsal room. Let them know that you will be choosing a Button for the process and that they should call Button any time they need to pause the process. Every time Button is called, the actor then must say what they need. Some examples:

- Button. Where does my hand go?

- Button. I need a minute to shake it out.

- Button. Can you remind me how long the kiss should be?

This tool is effective because it gives the actors a chance to breathe and something to say when their Fight-Flight-Freeze response takes over. Even in a positive and relaxed rehearsal environment, emotions can be heightened. If an actor has been fully engaged with a high-stakes scene, a simple logistical question might send them into survival mode. The Button gives everyone a way to work through that moment of panic.

In rehearsal, the actors remain in the moment, as they do when calling for "line," and then they can ask whatever question they need to ask, breathe for a second, or remind their partner of a boundary. Once they have what they need, the work continues. Functionally, the Button is a mini-hold or a "yellow-light" safeword. But hold is used to indicate physical safety or danger and the term "safeword" has real-life sexual implications, so both are to be avoided for general actor concerns. The Button normalizes needing to pause for a second and ask a question or adjust a boundary. Performers need that permission, and having a tool in place to support them will help your process and give them an established way to ask for what they need.

Games for Practicing "No" and Button

Two games, both variations on classics, can help the room get familiar with saying "Button."

Simon Says (with Some Twists)

One player is Simon. Simon gives instructions. If the instruction is prefaced by "Simon Says" the players should follow it, and without the preface, they do not.

Play a few rounds with the standard rules before you add the first twist: the participants at any time, for any reason, can choose not to comply with Simon's command, even if Simon "said." Instead, the participants return to neutral and say "no." The "no's" might be timid at first, or Simon might need to be tyrannical (ask the participants to pick their noses or their teeth) to get a "no" from your group. Or they might be a group that loves shouting "NO" right off the bat.

After playing a few rounds with the "no" option, ask the participants how it felt to say "no" to the person in charge. They may say it felt uncomfortable at first. Or that it made them feel powerful. Some might observe that after they say "no," nothing bad happened, which is, of course, the whole point. When "no" is the only alternative to "yes," it can feel risky to say.

As Simon, hearing even a tentative "no" can feel a lot like hearing "NO!" is being shouted at you. It can feel like your authority is being challenged, and not in a good way.

Now try twist two: This time, the players continue to have two choices when responding to a command. They can do the action, or they can return to neutral and say Button. After a few rounds, ask them how it felt to say Button. Participants often report that it was lower pressure to say Button than to say "No". Simon usually feels better about hearing the Button as well.

Button doesn't mean "no," so the third and final iteration of the twist is that after Button is called, the Button-caller offers a next step. Some examples:

Simon Says, "Touch both of your shoulders."

- Button! I'd like to try touching my left shoulder.

- Button! I need a minute.

- Button! Can we try something else?

Simon hears the offers and then gives the next direction to keep the game moving.

The Circle Game (or "Yes" with a Twist)

An acting class staple, again, with a twist. Participants stand in a circle facing one another. One player, Participant A, will begin the game by gesturing across the circle and seeking eye contact with another player, Participant B. Participant B will then say, "Yes." Upon receiving the "yes," Participant A moves across the circle to Participant B's spot. While Participant A is crossing, Participant B gestures to and seeks eye contact from Participant C. And so on.

The original game reinforces basic concepts like seeking eye contact, specificity, presence, and attentiveness. It also, unfortunately, reinforces the pre-existing idea that "yes" is the implied answer to any and all questions in a rehearsal space.

Now the twist. This time, when Participant A gestures to Participant B, Participant B has a choice: say "yes," or "Button." If Participant B says "yes," Participant A crosses. If Participant B says "Button," Participant A stays put. No matter what, Participant B has the next move. Participant B then gestures to someone, Participant C, and the game continues.

There will be a learning curve in this version. There is an occasional traffic jam when one participant comes to take a spot that hasn't been vacated, but the other participants simply make room in the circle and adjust. It becomes apparent, quickly, who is relying on assumptions or muscle memory to play the game instead of actually waiting to receive a "yes". Many participants will start moving the moment the other participant says anything, or even the moment they gesture. This twist helps teach participants to treat the gesture like an actual ask, not like a sure thing, and it also enforces the idea that the person giving the answer (yes or Button) is in charge of the next move. The final step is to have the gesturing participant ask what the button-caller needs. It shouldn't turn into a long improvisation. When the button-caller says Button, the gesturing participant asks, "What do you need?" The button-caller says, "I need this". Then, the button-caller and gesturing participant decide who should make the next gesture and the game continues.

Fences

The Boundary Practice is not so much Show, Don't Tell, as it is Show, *Then* Tell. A verbal boundary is easier than a physical one to write down in a script or prompt book and they are easier to have a quick conversation about. It is critical that the verbal boundary, or "Fence", reinforces a physically established boundary.

In the Boundary Practice, actors identify the boundaries their partner showed them physically by verbally describing the areas they physically were guided around. Those boundary lines are called Fences. For example, if Partner A didn't give Partner B permission to touch their left shoulder, they would make that physically clear during the Boundary Practice. Partner B would acknowledge and reinforce that boundary by saying, "I saw a Fence around your left shoulder." The image of a Fence allows the participants to imagine their partner's boundaries visually. "My partner didn't give me permission to touch their upper chest. They have a Fence around their upper chest."

In The Boundary Practice, when naming Fences, notice that the partner being shown the Fences names the Fences. The reasoning here is twofold. If Partner A knows their own boundaries, but Partner A didn't communicate them to Partner B in a way Partner B understands, then that will become clear when Partner B names Fences. The second reason is that if Partner A may accidentally indicate a Fence. If that happens, Partner A can catch it when Partner B names their Fences and then they can clarify. For example, lots of people don't give their partners permission to touch their faces during the Boundary Practice. Sometimes, that's because Partner A has a boundary around their face, or a specific part of their face. Sometimes, they don't touch their face because it seems obvious to Partner A that the face is fine to touch. If Partner B says, "I saw a fence around your face," Partner A would be able to confirm or clarify what they meant to indicate.

When naming Fences, keep the names for body parts neutral. Remember, what you might call a part of your partner's body might not be how they refer to that part of themselves. What you would call breasts, your partner may call something else. Here are some neutral examples of commonly Fenced areas:

- Front of upper chest
- Front of pelvis
- Back of Pelvis

Other common spots for Fences:

- Upper, inner thigh
- Back of neck
- Armpits
- Eyes
- Glasses
- Hair

TOOLS AND TECHNIQUES   23

Try not to take Fences personally. If you got into the habit of referring to the fence in front of your neighbor's house as an anti-neighbor barrier, you might feel offended by the fence. You might feel offended and confused about what you did wrong to have that neighbor put that boundary up. But to your neighbor, it might just be a fence. It might look nice, protect their kids while they play in the yard, or keep the dog from running away. That fence isn't about anyone but your neighbor and their preferences and needs. Like your neighbor's fence, these Fences were there long before you got there and are about your partner, not you.

Rather than saying, "You can't touch here," which feels a little bit like it might have something to do with the prospective toucher in this method, say, "I have a Fence here." The Fence just is.

Gates

Fences may have Gates. Sometimes an actor is unwilling to give general permission to their partner to touch them in a particular area of their body, but depending on the context of the touch, they may be circumstantially open to it. This is called Opening a Gate.

The simplest example of Opening a Gate might be front of body contact in a hug. A lot of actors have Fences around the fronts of their pelvises and the front of their upper chest. They might not want their partner's hands or faces going into those areas, but if those actors were interested in trying a hug in a scene, can say, "What do you think about Opening the Gates on the fronts of our bodies to try a hug?" This is language for having conversations about boundaries and boundary negotiations that is a part of ongoing boundary check in's throughout the production process. Don't throw Boundaries out the window and say, "Oh, it's just a hug." Don't disregard boundaries just because the physical action doesn't seem intimate. The boundaries you are establishing are about touch, intimate or otherwise. Gates give you a tool to talk about it.

During casting, an actor may agree to particular moments of touch or intimacy. That moment of touch in the script may be the only time that actor is open to that touch. That can be made clear by having the area Fenced-off during the Boundary Practice and then the Gates can be opened by the actor at the appropriate time. That Gate may not be ready to be opened the first days of rehearsal, so discuss the Gate with the actors and put the staging of that moment on the schedule in a spot that works for everyone. An actor's Fence is the Fence and permission to open and close the Gate is entirely the decision of the actor. Later on, in the Boundary Practice, you will see how it works when an actor is willing to open Gates for one partner and not for another.

THE BOUNDARY PRACTICE

Button, Fences, and Gates all come together in The Boundary Practice.

The basic version of this practice is for two partners. Before beginning, be sure to introduce the Button (no need to introduce Fences and Gates before the exercise). Have the partners choose who will be Partner A and who will be Partner B.

1. Partners begin facing each other in an open, neutral body position. This can be done sitting or standing.

2. Partner A will begin at the top of their head and will begin showing by touching everywhere that they are giving their partner permission to touch today. This is done without speaking.

    a. Partner A should go slowly and use wiping, sliding, or smoothing motions, rather than patting motions. Patting can be hard to follow.
    b. If Partner A needs to bend over or turn around to show Partner B where they are giving permission to be touched on the back of their body, they should do so. Partner B can also move around Partner A to see the back of Partner A's body.
    c. If there is an area that Partner A is unable to reach, but that they would like to give permission to Partner B to touch, they can indicate those areas by pointing to them.

3. After that step is complete, Partner A asks Partner B "Would it work for me to take your hands?" If they get a yes, Partner A then takes Partner B's

hands and brings them onto Partner A's body, touching everywhere Partner A gave Partner B permission to touch.

   a. If Partner B said "no," or Button to having their hands taken, see Boundary Practice Modification.
   b. At any time, if Partner B's hands are going somewhere they prefer not to touch, they can say Button. If Partner B says Button, Partner B then says where they would like to continue from. This step gets them in physical contact with each other, but the first time Partner B touches Partner A, both of them have had a say in it.

4. After Partner A has guided Partner B over everywhere that they are giving Partner B permission to touch, Partner B names Partner A's Fences.

   If Partner A didn't take B's hands over their upper chest, Partner B would say, "I saw a Fence around your upper chest." After Partner B names all of the Fences that they saw, they should ask if they missed any. Then Partner A has an opportunity to clarify anything that Partner B missed, or that Partner A unintentionally added.

5. Flip the exercise. Partner B shows, asks, takes A over everywhere they give permission, Partner A uses Button as needed, Partner A names Partner B's Fences, and then Partner B can clarify.

The partners repeat the exercise as many times as needed so that all partners for a particular scene are familiar with each other's boundaries. Many scenes will have two partners, but sometimes a scene or show will have many more pairings. Boundaries will vary from pair to pair or from group to group. For example, Partner A might be very comfortable with Partner B touching their thigh, but may not give Partner C permission to do so. Take the time to let all pairs run through the exercise.

If you have scenes with more than two people, you can cycle everyone through the Boundary Practice two-by-two or you can try the Group Boundary Practice.

Boundary Practice Modification

The modification begins after Partner A has shown Partner B everywhere they are giving Partner B permission to touch them today. When Partner A asks if it would work for Partner B for them to take B's hands, if Partner B says no, try the modification. Rather than taking Partner B's hands, Partner A will repeat step one again, showing their partner everywhere that they're giving their partner permission to touch today. As Partner A shows again, Partner B has three options: they can follow with their hand behind Partner A's hand, hover over Partner A's hand, or place their hand on top of Partner A's hand. All three options communicate the permission to touch without the need to manipulate Partner B's hands.

After Partner A has shown Partner B again, Partner B will name Partner A's Fences, as in the original exercise.

Similar to the original exercise, at any point any of the partners can lift their hands or say Button and then resume. Partner B rejoins wherever works for them.

Someone may not want their hands managed for a variety of reasons, from wrist injuries to sweaty palms, but this modification takes that preference into account.

What to Say: The First Time through the Boundary Practice

Here's a version of talking a pair of partners through The Boundary Practice for the first time.
"There is some physical contact and intimacy in this show, so let's take a few minutes and establish some boundaries. A good boundary is a clear boundary, so I'm going to take us through a little exercise to give us good, clear information to work with while we work together.

(Continued)

28 TOOLS AND TECHNIQUES

"Before we start the exercise, I want to introduce you all to our version of 'hold' for this process: the Button. It's the pause Button for our process. As we are working, if you have any questions or need to communicate something with your partner, go ahead and say Button.

"I'm going to be talking a whole bunch through this, but I'm not doing anything interesting, so stay focused on your partner.

"Sitting or standing, face your partner. Pick a Partner A and pick a Partner B. Soft ankles, knees, and hips. Breathe. See if you can allow your lips to part. Find that neutral balance. See each other. Let the talking fall away.

"Partner A: with your own hands on your own body, starting at the top of your head and working all the way down to your feet, show by touching everywhere on your body that you are giving Partner B permission to touch today. Go slowly and be specific. If you need to bend over, or point to a place you can't reach, or turn around to show them, go ahead. Partner B, you are observing.

"Now Partner A, ask Partner B if it works for you to take their hands. If you get a yes, Partner A takes Partner B's hands. If you get a no or your partner says Button, raise your hand and I will give you an alternative. (Offer Boundary Practice Modification)

"Partner B, in this next step, remember you can say Button at any time because your hands are a part of your body. Partner A, take Partner B's hands and starting at the top of your head and working all the way down to your feet, guide Partner B's hands over everywhere on your body that you are giving them permission to touch today. If your partner says Button, pause, lift their hands, and find the next place to resume the exercise. Go slowly and be specific. If you need to bend over, or point to a place you can't reach, or turn around to show them, go ahead.

"When you finish, return to facing each other in a neutral position and Partner B, name the areas that Partner A guided you away from and didn't give you permission to touch. The way that we name those boundaries is by naming your partner's Fences. For example, 'I saw a fence around your upper chest. I saw a fence around the front of your pelvis, etc.' Be specific and use neutral language. Then ask, 'Did I miss anything?'

"Partner A can then clarify if you missed or added any Fences.

"Now, let's reverse it.

"Partner B: with your own hands on your own body, starting at the top of your head and working all the way down to your feet, show by touching everywhere on your body that you are giving Partner A permission to touch today. Go slowly and be specific. If you need to bend over, or point to a place you can't reach, or turn around to show them, go ahead. Partner A, you are observing.

"Now Partner B, ask Partner A if it works for you to take their hands. If you get a yes, Partner A takes Partner B's hands. If you get a no, raise your hand and I will give you an alternative. (Offer Boundary Practice Modification)

"Remember you can say Button at any time because your hands are a part of your body. If your partner says Button, pause, lift their hands, and find the next place to resume the exercise. Partner B, take Partner A's hands and starting at the top of your head and working all the way down to your feet, guide Partner A's hands over everywhere on your body that you are giving them permission to touch today. Go slowly and be specific. If you need to bend over, or point to a place you can't reach, or turn around to show them, go ahead.

"When you finish, return to neutral and Partner A, name the areas that Partner B guided you away from and didn't give you permission to touch. The way that we name those boundaries is to say that you saw a fence around that area. For example, 'I saw a fence around your chest. I saw a fence around the front of your pelvis, etc.' Be specific and use neutral language. Then ask, 'Did I miss anything?'

"Partner B can then clarify if you missed or added any Fences.

"Before we work on any of the scenes with intimacy, I'll give you time to go through this again, but you can revisit this exercise at any time with your partner."

Group Boundary Practice

If boundaries need to be established for group intimacy, high-touch scenes, or as a general practice in a production or class, another option is to do a Group Boundary Practice. Group Boundary Practice is not a replacement for the Boundary Practice, but a supplement exercise that allows the touch in boundary establishment to better reflect the conditions of the touch that may be experienced in the performance.

30 TOOLS AND TECHNIQUES

The reasoning behind practicing group boundary establishment this way rather than having every single person partner with every single other person is two-fold. One, the experience of having 20 hands on you at once, even if they're all in places you've given them permission to be, can be an overwhelming experience, and that's useful to find out during boundary establishment, rather than in a heightened state during rehearsal. If an actor has given everyone in the group individually permission to touch their stomach and their back, that may be well within their boundaries when there are only two hands on them. When they have the opportunity to consider that there will be 20 hands on them because they are working with ten partners in a scene, their boundaries may be different.

The second reason is because this allows for individuals to ask about opening Gates without giving general permission to the group to touch in Fenced-off areas. Partners face each other.

1. Partner A indicates on their hand with touching themselves using smoothing, sliding, or wiping motions everywhere they are giving their partners permission to touch today.

2. Partner A repeats step one, showing Partner B, C, D, E, etc., everywhere they are giving those partners permission to touch today. Partners A, B, C, D, E, etc., follow along behind Partner A's hand, creating a train of hands. As Partner A's hand moves up their arm, Partner B's hand follows behind, followed by C, D, E, etc.

3. Then the group then verbally reinforces Partner A's boundaries by naming Partner A's Fences. Partner A can then clarify.

4. Showing partner rotates until all members of the group have shown all other members their boundaries.

Quick Check-Ins

Do you need to do the Boundary Practice every time you work, or before every rehearsal? Yes and no. No, you don't need to go through the entire Boundary Practice every time you're going to do an exercise, even though the Boundary Practice only takes three minutes once it starts running smoothly. Once actors have done the full Boundary Practice with their partners, they can do a Fence Check-in. In a Fence Check-in, actors can remind each other of their Fences that day, or they can ask their partners if they have any new Fences. This shorthand for checking in reminds the actors of their boundaries, but it also reinforces that their boundaries can shift and change. As a director, you can prompt the actors to do a Fence Check-in. In a classroom setting, everyone can go around the circle and name their Fences.

TOOLS AND TECHNIQUES **31**

Navigating Resistance

Sometimes actors are resistant to trying the Boundary Practice. An actor may think it's silly or unnecessary and that can put a lot of pressure on their partner to shrug it off too.

Actors occasionally push to skip Boundary Practice because they feel comfortable with "anything." Encourage them to participate in the exercise anyway because even if they "don't need it," it is a valuable tool for their toolkit and a necessary part of a consent-based process.

- Tell actors to try it as a character development exercise.

  You might be "down for whatever" but your partner is playing your daughter/you are in a particular historical period your character has this particular trait. Let's find your character's boundaries with each other.

- Tell them it's for your information so you can choreograph the scenes later.

- Tell them you are working on learning a new technique, this is a part of your process, and you need to practice.

PLACEHOLDERS

One of the simplest tools in the staging intimacy toolkit is the Placeholder, and it is an important one to introduce before getting into any staging. The Placeholder is a high-five. Where there would be an intimate moment (or even a moment of violence) have the actors high-five or bring their palms together. If the moment is a solo intimate moment, use a clap, much the same way dancers mark turns in rehearsal.

For a number of reasons, a director might find themselves unable to stage or rehearse intimacy on any given day. An actor might be sick, or they are running out of time and just want to get through the end of the scene, or maybe they want to brush up on the protocol outlined in this book before you tackle a scene. Maybe actors want to do a Boundary Practice check-in and there isn't time. High-five.

Intentionally low-stakes and casual, introducing the high-five Placeholder communicates three important things:

- Something goes here.

A scene blocked without intimacy can feel disrupted when you get back to it later. This keeps it fresh in everyone's minds that there is something getting plugged in here and lets them know you haven't forgotten about it.

- Whatever goes here isn't a big deal.

One of the challenges of staging intimacy is that so many actors have had really bad, overly sexualized experiences. A high-five, an intentionally un-sexy casual gesture, lets the actors know that whatever happens there won't be weird. Actors can get as serious or as goofy as they want about their high-five. What matters is that it's not drenched in psychologically serious or sexual language. Rather than starting the scene, calling hold, reminding the actors that the big, currently unstaged and mysterious intimate moment happens there, and then asking them to restart the scene, the actors merely high-five, and keep playing the scene.

- Placeholders are always available in rehearsal.

The week before tech, if an actor is sick and just isn't up for the big intimate moment, they can always return to the Placeholder, even after the moment is staged. Sick actors (and their partners) love the Placeholder. Even if in the moment you decide to use a Placeholder, just hold up your hand when your partner goes in for the kiss. High-five and move on. No explanation needed.

Early in the process, introduce the ensemble to The Placeholder to keep handling theatrical intimacy from holding up your process and help the actors to take control of their work day-to-day. Early on, the Placeholders may be quick high-fives, but as the work develops, the Placeholders may change in duration or become more complex to signify the intention of the gesture that will eventually go in that space. A long, lingering Placeholder may indicate a long, lingering embrace and a quick tap might be for a peck on the cheek. Playing the intention of the scene doesn't have to wait for choreography.

DE-ROLING

A valuable tool for maintaining emotional boundaries is De-Roling. Versions of De-roling appear in several acting pedagogies, notably in the work of Augusto Boal; it's helpful in intimacy work for maintaining separation between the truth of the scene and the reality of real life. De-roling is a simple, but powerful tool for getting separation between actor and character. In De-roling, the actor states as the character what they're doing, both physically, emotionally, what they're saying or what lines of text they're speaking, and maybe even how they're feeling. Then they say, "But as the actor," and they say what the actor has been doing physically, emotionally, verbally.

> Here's an example of what De-roling might sound like:
>
> In my experience as my character, I am shoving you and abusing you and manipulating you and making you afraid because I am seeking revenge, and I'm calling you hateful names. But as the actor, I am doing my choreography. I'm Opening and Closing Distance. I'm seeking Eye Contact, and I am speaking the words of the playwright, and I would never say these things to you in real life.

This can be done as a partnered exercise or it can be used solo. It's important to process the differences out loud because it helps create distance, much in the same way talking about a breakup is cathartic.

De-roling can also be a useful technique when staging scenes with any kind of traumatic content. De-roling helps both offerers and recipients of theatrically violent narratives take a step back from the scene.

While de-roling was intended to be used by performers, it's also proven valuable for leaders in processes. It can be helpful for the director to take a step back and say, "To tell the story of this play, we are doing X and Y and Z."

In this play, I am asking you to do X and Y and Z, but as the director, I'm using this technique and this technique and best practices for staging intimacy to tell the story the playwright gave us, or to tell the story that we've created as an ensemble.

It's not only helpful for getting some emotional distance from violent or aggressive content, but De-roling is also useful for preventing "showmance." If an actor is in an intense romantic scene with another actor, they may want to take some space at the end of rehearsal and say,

As the character I'm in love with you. I feel open and vulnerable to you. We have a lot of chemistry, and I'm feeling such strong feelings, that to my character, they seem out of control. As the actor, I'm practicing vulnerability using my technique. I'm using intimacy choreography language, I'm speaking the words of the playwright, and using my imagination.

This can help break down the illusion that what's happening in the rehearsal space is real, and it can help to preserve a more professional working environment for the company.

STOP STEPPING IN

Intimacy choreography is different from other types of staging. In a fight or dance scene, it is established professional practice that the choreographer might need to ask for consent to step in to demonstrate a move or sequence. Due to the sensitive nature of intimate physical contact, the specificity of the established boundaries, and the power dynamic inherent in a director/choreographer to actor relationship, it is inappropriate to step into an intimate scene to demonstrate.

This is one of the most common mistakes that people make when staging intimacy. Even if a director or choreographer thinks the actors are comfortable with them, they are still the person in power. When stepping into a scene, they are teaching the actors that they are working with that the boundaries they have carefully established with each other don't matter if the person with the power tries to cross them. That's a bad message for any actor to internalize.

Maintaining physical distance is important in this work. Stepping in includes making contact, but also reaching between, or over, an actor. Work instead in a parallel lane to the actors. Think about a pane of glass between the director and the actors. There is a clear delineation between their actor space and director space.

Also try and avoid miming any of the sexual gestures or demonstrating the choreography on an assistant. Instead, use the clear, descriptive, desexualized language from later in this book to stage the scene. Respect the boundaries the actors have established and direct and choreograph from the side.

BOUNDARY BREAKERS

To deal with boundary breakers, you first need to establish clear boundaries. Not only physical boundaries established between actors, but professional boundaries established in the process. It is important to the integrity of the process that everyone abides by those boundaries- including the director.

No matter how comfortable an ensemble might be, it's important for the boundaries and expectations to be explicit so that everyone can be on the same page and held accountable. If someone's crossing a line, the first step in addressing that boundary breaking is to have a conversation with the people in question.

If you are the leader in the process, and the boundary crossing is something you personally noticed, you can address it with the person directly. If the issue is brought to your attention by a third party, have a conversation with the actor whose boundaries are perceived as being crossed first.

Because the actors have tools to establish and reestablish their own boundaries, those actors may have renegotiated boundaries without the director being aware of it. Before you jump all over Juliet for crossing Romeo's boundaries, check in with Romeo to see how the work is going because they may have reestablished boundaries without you knowing.

If there is a problem, try to refer to "crossing" rather than "violating" boundaries. The terms have different implications, and one can feel a lot more confrontational than the other. Check in with the other actor and say, "hey, it's come to my attention that during some of the work on the scene (be specific about when the boundary crossing is happening) that some of your physical choices are crossing your partner's boundaries. I'd like to take a little bit of time before you run the next scene and review the Boundary Practice". Run the Boundary Practice, ask if there are any questions, and move on with rehearsal as planned.

As soon as possible, document the discussion. Document the nature of the issue, how it was brought to your attention, what conversations you had about it and how those conversations went. Whenever possible, have that conversation with somebody else present.

36 TOOLS AND TECHNIQUES

If boundary crossing continues, having clear documentation of the incident, when you address the incidents, how you address the incidents, and how those conversations went can be helpful in resolving your issue, either through recasting or through a different kind of disciplinary measure. Having a company policy, or a clause in the actor's contracts about boundary breaking can also support you in determining the appropriate path forward.

If you've had a conversation about boundary crossing and they've had an opportunity to establish boundaries with their partner, and they are continuing to cross boundaries, that's a situation where recasting is entirely appropriate. Make sure that you are in conversation with the artistic staff at the theatre or the administration at the university where you're working.

JOKING AROUND

Often, at times, to lighten the mood, actors will make sexual or inappropriate comments. When it's coming from the actors it can feel like you shouldn't stop them if it seems to make them comfortable. But even if the jokes make the actors comfortable, it's important to maintain a desexualized environment. Rather than just telling actors to stop, encourage actors to speak about the choreography in terms of the language or talk about it as their characters. *"As Stanley, I am x y and z"*, rather than, *"I, Bob, want to get into your pants."*

If they're not talking about the choreography and are making more inappropriate jokes and comments, reminding the team that rehearsal is a professional environment can go a long way. Encourage everyone to keep that sort of behavior outside of the rehearsal room, not just when the group is working but also when on breaks. Sexualized joking can promote an uncomfortable environment, especially for people who are wanting to be collegial and supportive but don't feel comfortable participating in the jokes.

ADDITIONAL BOUNDARIES

A lot of directors want their theatrical rehearsal processes to feel like everyone's a family, that everyone is connected and engaged with each other, that the process is respectful and collaborative, and that everyone is all in it together. That's wonderful. Ensembles might warm up together or do conditioning work together, and sometimes the director joins in on that opportunity to support eachother collegially.

When it comes to rehearsing intimacy, nudity, or sexual violence, collective acts of solidarity are not appropriate. Morale does not improve when the director (or non-involved actors) get naked in solidarity. This may seem obvious, but more than one overly-enthusastic ensemble, including the director, has tried it. Regardless of how comfortable you think your cast is with you, regardless of how comfortable you think it would make everyone if you were all on the same playing field and they got to see you naked, too, remember that's not what they consented to. It's not what they signed on for, and it's not serving our purposes of creating a desexualized rehearsal environment

Beyond remaining clothed in rehearsal, there are a few other personal boundaries to consider. There may be existing personal and professional relationships between people on a production. Establishing a work-time and social-time boundary provides structure to behavioral expectations when spouses, friends, and families are in the rehearsal room. Define those boundaries at the first meeting and clarify what they mean. Here are some examples of Work-Time and Social-Time boundaries:

Work-Time (when you treat each other as co-workers)

- When you get to the theatre.

- When we are talking about the play or rehearsal (in-person, via email, over text).

- From the auditions through closing night.

Social-Time (when you treat each other as real-life friends/lovers/spouses)

- Post-rehearsal meals

- Break time

- Closing night

Acknowledging an existing personal relationship is often the simplest and most straightforward thing to do. If everyone knows an actor and the director are married and they never mention it, it can feel weird. But acknowledgement of existing relationship doesn't mean that Work-Time boundaries shouldn't be respected by everyone.

MAKING MISTAKES

Mistakes happen. An accidental touch or an accidental sexualization of a direction can feel like a major catastrophe in the pressure cooker of a rehearsal process.

When mistakes happen, addressing the mistake directly is often the best way to move forward. It doesn't need to be a long, drawn out post mortem, but it keeps the process moving in a way that makes everyone feel respected. A good post-mistake conversation can follow the structure of this four-part apology:

1. Own your mistakes

Tell them that you messed up. Don't sugar coat it. If it is about one moment, name the moment.

I touched you without asking.

It is important to establish boundary expectations early in the process, but it is also important to acknowledge the expectations have not been met. If this is a situation where someone brings your boundary crossing to your attention in week three of rehearsal, an itemized list of your wrongdoing might not be productive. Instead, address your general issue.

It has been brought to my attention that I have been crossing boundaries throughout this process.

2. Apologize

Most of the mistakes conscientious directors make are unintentional. Regardless of your intentions, it's important to apologize when you make mistakes or cross boundaries. Say you're sorry. It's important.

I'm sorry about that./I apologize.

In a situation where you have wronged someone, it can be tempting to explain your intentions. I encourage you to leave your intentions out. If you told an inappropriate joke, it doesn't matter that you were trying to be funny and lighten up an awkward moment. What matters is that it was inappropriate.

3. Thank them

Remind them that their boundaries benefit everyone and that it helps you grow when you get called on your mistakes. Actors can feel like they need to apologize for their own boundaries, as if they are an inconvenience. This helps them let that go and feel empowered in the process.

This might feel corny or insincere, but this can take a variety of forms.

Thank you for helping me become more aware of touch in my practice.

I'm working on this and I appreciate you raising my awareness.

Making sure this space is a positive and productive one is important to me, and even though it is hard to hear, I'm grateful for the feedback.

This will help me be a better director. Thanks.

4. Figure out the way forward

Is it a one time thing that is unlikely to happen again? Take a break and get back to work. Is this a repeat offense? Acknowledge that and come up with a plan for making sure this is the last time. Do you need to have a full cast discussion? Make time for it. Offer to have a larger discussion or to bring someone further up the chain so that the cast understands that you are holding yourself responsible. Ask them what they need.

Do you need anything? Do we want to take a five and get back to it? Thanks!

If handled well, mistakes are a learning opportunity for the whole cast. Brushed off or handled poorly, they can tank a process. Take responsibility and make doing better an active part of your work. Your ensemble will appreciate it.

CHAPTER 2

The Ingredients

Actors standing on stage, consensually, efficiently establishing boundaries with each other isn't what most people think of when they think about staging theatrical intimacy. It may not be particularly compelling and probably isn't worth the price of a ticket. The ups and downs, gasps and grabs telling the story of an intimate moment are why we bother staging intimacy in the first place. The choreography is where the story lies.

The challenge is to avoid all of the pitfalls of the old approaches for choreography and to keep the process desexualized. How do you ask for a passionate make-out on the couch without asking for a passionate make-out on the couch? Or a position change in a long, complicated, comedic sex scene? How do you tweak what the actors find organically? What is the language for recording everything you found so it isn't lost to rehearsals past? Desexualizing the process and not stepping in can feel like major barriers. If you aren't supposed to demonstrate, and you can't just describe what you want to happen using normal "sexual" language, how do you stage intimacy?

The Ingredients are the desexualized vocabulary for describing intimate movement and your tools for crafting the story. How we talk about staging intimacy is as important as what we stage.

In developing a vocabulary specifically for staging intimacy, I pulled vocabulary from a wide range of artistic disciplines, including dance, physical theatre, and visual art. Each of The Ingredients is very simple, but they are intended to be used in combinations, like Ingredients in a recipe, to suit your particular taste. They are each discrete parts of a whole, but they work in any number of Recipes. Just like cooking, it's in the combinations where the magic happens.

There are ten Ingredients:

1. Opening and Closing Distance
2. Levels of Touch
3. Tempo and Counts

(Continued)

4. Shapes
5. Destination
6. Eye Contact
7. Visible Power Shifts
8. Breath and Sound
9. Gravity and Weight
10. Kissing

The Ingredients are meant to be combined and get a little more advanced as you go. Let's look at them one by one and then look at how they can be combined to stage a range of intimate scenes.

OPENING AND CLOSING DISTANCE

The first Ingredient that we're going to look at is Opening and Closing Distance. This is very similar to the language that's found in other movement and performance pedagogies. Actors usually understand this Ingredient without any special intimacy-focused introduction.

We use Opening and Closing Distance in three different ways.

1. To describe the space between bodies or objects and changes in that space. For example, if Partner A walks towards Partner B, we would say that Partner A is Closing Distance with Partner B. Partner A can also close the Distance between themselves and the couch.

2. To describe the Distance between a body part and either another body part or element in space and the changes in that distance. For example, Partner B can close the distance between their nose and Partner A's shoulder. Partner A could also open the Distance between their own knees. Partner A can close the distance between their shoulder and the wall.

3. To describe how the distance opens and closes. For example, Partner A can push Partner B away by opening the distance between them with their hands.

The movement can be isolated (just Partner A closes the distance with their lips) or multiple opening and closing motions can happen at the same time (Partner A closes the distance with their lips while Partner B opens the distance with their hands.)

Let's practice this Ingredient.

THE INGREDIENTS **41**

> *Opening and Closing Hands*
>
> Holding your hands out in front of yourself, palms facing each other, imagine that each of your hands is a partner in a scene. Try these to get a feel for it and then see what sorts of stories you can interpret just by Opening and Closing the Distance between your hands.
>
> - Keep your left hand still, slowly bring your right hand to it. After your hands touch, have your right hand slowly open to the starting position.
> - Keep your left hand still, repeat the slow close from the right hand. After your hands touch, have your left hand open.
> - Closing the distance with your right hand, while simultaneously closing with your left.
> - Closing the distance with your left hand, and right before the hands touch, open distance with your right hand.
>
> Make up a few combinations of your own and see if you can add story or character to them.

Telling Stories

Now imagine you are working on a scene and you were going to tell the story through distance. What would the pattern be? Who closes, who opens, and when? Just with your hands, try staging:

- A seduction.

- A warm reunion after a year apart.

- A the end of a first date. Kiss or shake hands?

- A long, difficult goodbye.

When working on a scene, have the actors just tell the story through the opening and closing distance with each other. Have them work with no contact or with the Placeholder to get the shape of the scene. In intimate scenes, often the distance between the bodies closes and then there are smaller openings and closings that create the image of sexual gestures and contact.

Directing Distance

Here are some examples of how this Ingredient might sound in rehearsal.

- As you pull back and open distance between your chests, can you close the distance between your pelvises?

- Can you close the distance between your torso and your partner's back?

- Can you open distance as she tries to close distance?

- When you close the distance between your nose and his inner thigh, can you also close the distance with your chin?

LEVELS OF TOUCH

Different touches tell different stories, and the amount of pressure in the touch communicates a lot of information. To describe that pressure, we are going to break touch down into three levels of touch. To keep things desexualized with levels of touch, we don't caress our partners. We find Skin and Muscle level touch where our partners have given us permission to touch today.

Each of the levels can be used to tell a wide range of stories and each level has three names. The first name is the anatomical name. Skin, Muscle, and Bone levels of touch refer to the anatomical features we imagine we are pressing into.

For some artists, it is easier to imagine that they are tracing lightly, painting smoothly, or shaping their partner's body with the pressure. If that visual is more clear, we can use the "art supply" names for each of the levels. Skin, Muscle, and Bone correspond to Powder, Paint, and Clay.

For artists who might not respond to metaphor, try Touching, Moving, and Pulling. You are touching your partner (or their clothes), moving your partner (or

THE INGREDIENTS   **43**

their clothes), or pulling your partner (or their clothes). Use whichever one makes the most sense to you and the artists you are working with.

Let's take a look at finding each level and how you might use them.

Level 1: Skin/Powder/Touching

With your own hand, on your arm, trace your fingers along the skin. Feel that sensation. Now imagine you are tracing a fine powder over the skin. Use your fingertips, the back of your hand, and your palm to explore Level 1 touch.

Now try it on a section of wall. Close distance with the wall and make Level 1 touch with your fingertips, then with your shoulder, then hip, and then your thigh. Keep the contact light.

Level 1 touch is great for a variety of different intimate moments. To desexualize the process, try asking for Level 1 touch instead of asking the actors to be:

Gentle	Familial	Nervous
Tender	Calming	Creepy
Loving	Unsure	Controlling
Sweet	Hesitant	Manipulative
Excited	Soothing	Predatory

The right column of the list might be surprising, but it all depends on the context of the scene and the location of the contact. Level 1 touch to trace the side of a partner's face is different from that same touch to their inner thigh, just as skin level contact to the stomach can be comforting and loving or very creepy.

Level 2: Muscle/Paint/Moving

With your own hand, on your own arm, think into the muscles of your arm. Level 2 touch is a little bit heavier, and there is more friction between the fingers and the skin. You're thinking into the muscles, not trying to grab the muscles. The skin or sleeve of your shirt moves with the friction. Try thinking about painting your arm with thick paint. The pressure might be similar to a massage, but there isn't necessarily the kneading motion. Try making Level 2 touch with your palms on your thighs or with your shoulder on your cheek.

Try asking for Level 2 touch instead of asking the actors to be:

Romantic	Needy	Powerful
Passionate	Intense	Insistent
Loving	Turned-on	Forceful
Protective	Hot and Heavy	Controlling
Urgent	Gropey	Aggressive

(Continued)

Level 3: Bone/Clay/Pulling

This is the deepest level of contact, so rather than trying to actually touch bone, actors should *think* into their partner's bones. It's an imaginative connection. It's about telling the story of bone deep connection, not about actually making bone deep connection. It's a small but important distinction that can make a big difference in preventing bruising.

   With your own hand, on your own arm, think into your bones. Imagine you can feel them. Imagine you are molding clay. Imagine you are pushing or pulling your body or your clothing with your touch. Try Level 3 touch when you are looking for touch that tells stories about characters who are:

Passionate	Overwhelmed	Loving
Needy	Powerful	Urgent
Hungry	Dangerous	Violent
Raw	Intense	Aggressive
Desperate	Forceful	Terrified
Protective	Controlling	Afraid

   Sometimes people shy away from Level 3 touch because it can seem too intense. The level of touch is deeper, but the depth and character intensity aren't necessarily the same thing.

Tips for Using Levels of Touch

- Introduce the Levels.

While Opening and Closing Distance might not need any preface before you use it in rehearsal, this Ingredient works best with a short introduction. Have the actors find Skin/Powder/Touching, Muscle/Paint/Moving, and Bone/Clay/Pulling on their own arms. Have them try those levels of touch on a piece of furniture (like the back of a chair) before jumping in. A 60-second introduction will give you a very workable common vocabulary, not just for intimate scenes, but for describing all kinds of contact.

- Use different body parts.

It can be tempting to think about touch as a hand-focused behavior. But some of the most interesting touch options don't involve the hands at all. Skin level touch with the shoulder. Paint with the hip. Clay level touch between Partner A's face and Partner B's thigh.

- Don't be afraid to adjust.

The levels of touch are subjective, and actors will respond differently to them. What one actor thinks is skin level contact, you might perceive as muscle level contact, or maybe even bone level contact. If an actor that has a heavy skin level touch, you might want to avoid directing them to use Bone level contact because their enthusiasm might be too deep. If an actor is trying to do muscle level touch and it looks more like skin, ask them to try and think into their partner's bones. Shift to the "art supply" direction, or to the Touching, Moving, Pulling directions.

- Keep it moving (or don't)

The levels of touch can be dynamic (moving around) or static (still). If things are getting too wiggly, ask for some static touch. Too stiff? Ask them to keep the point of contact moving.

- Mix it up

Differences in levels of touch creates an interesting tension between characters. We learn a lot about a character by how they touch the world and the people in it. Encourage your actors to play with different levels to find the best way to tell the story. Mix and match levels until you get the desired effect. Partner A opening distance with Level 3 touch and Partner B closing distance with Level 1 touch can tell an interesting story.

- It's not just for touching people.

The levels of touch are great for tweaking how actors handle their partners, but also how they handle props and scenic elements. Looking for an actor to barely perch on the edge of a chair? Powder level touch with the furniture.

- Let it shift

It can feel unnatural to keep a touch just at one level. Over the duration of the touch, play with having it shift lighter or heavier to tell the story.

Try Levels of Touch on your own. Using a wall or tabletop:

- Close the distance between your fingertips and the surface, making skin level contact
- Open the distance for a breath and then close distance again, using your palms to make muscle level contact
- Shift that contact to bone level, thinking into the "bones" of that surface
- Shift to skin
- Back to muscle

Choreographing with Levels of Touch

Lots of awkward moments can be cleaned up with just the first two Ingredients. Here are examples of how this Ingredient sounds in rehearsal:

46 THE INGREDIENTS

- When your hands are on his back, can you give me muscle level touch with your fingertips? Think into their muscles with your fingers. You're moving their shirt around with your touch.

- Can you close that distance with bone level touch? Using Level 3 touch to close the distance? Pulling your partner to you?

- When you stroke their hair, can you try powder level touch? Just barely touching.

- Try shaping each other like clay and let the contact shift from point to point. It's not a static touch. Keep it moving.

TEMPO AND COUNTS

If you are looking to preserve your choreography or direction, or trying to capture a beautiful moment that happened organically, try counting it.

It can feel counterintuitive to assign counts to a performance when we put so much emphasis on following impulse. But even when we are following impulses, we still have to do the blocking, find our light, and say the words of the playwright. An actor's internal clock is a beautiful, but unpredictable thing.

If it seems unnatural to count out a kiss, consider that lighting designers program the lights to fade over a certain duration. Counts are already built into our world. Counting ensures that everything happens when it's supposed to. It ensures that a peck stays a peck and a long, deep kiss doesn't get rushed. It also allows expectations to be established. If you are choreographing a kiss (more on kissing later), it is necessary to determine the length of the kiss before the actors go for it.

Find your rhythm. Count in your head with a steady pace from one to five. Tap your foot to it. That internal rhythm is the key to using counts in your process. Counts, like all of the other Ingredients, have a number of uses depending on your style. Use Tempo directions (faster or slower) to speed things up and slow them down, then lock them in with counts.

Trying Counts

Pick a spot in the room with you that's six or seven feet away. Close that distance over two counts. You probably have to move fairly quickly. What if you close that same distance over 12 counts? How does that change the story? You can use tempo and counts to describe one partner's motion, two partners' motions in relationship to each other, or a partner's relationship to a piece of furniture. Closing the distance between an actor's back and the wall over a two-count is very different than letting that same gesture take seven or eight counts.

Beyond choreography, counts are an easy and quick way to tweak actor choices. If a hug in a scene looks a little rushed, you can say "that looked like a five or six count hug. Could we try a ten count hug with a three count open afterward?"

Rather than grab their partner and pull them in over a four count, you can ask the actors to close distance over a one count. If you like what they come up with, counts make that change easy to document.

Now try documenting a small tweak with counts. Make a cross from one point in the room to another. Count how long it takes. Write that down. Now add three counts (if it was five, now it is an eight). Make the cross again with the adjusted counts. It's slower, but a very specific amount slower. Now add one more count and make the cross a third time. How does that single count tweak the cross? It might seem like too much specificity, too precise, but when the moment being counted is a hand on a sensitive body part, or a moment of nudity, or a kiss, precision matters quite a bit.

Putting It Together

Let's combine our first three Ingredients. Here are a few mini-Recipes that play with counts for you to try on your own.

- Start a few feet from your chair. Over five counts, close distance with to the chair and make skin/powder level contact for five counts. Open over a one.

- Now, start a few feet from your chair. Over eight counts, close distance with to the chair and make skin/powder level contact for two counts. Open over ten counts.

- Start in contact the chair. Using muscle level touch, leading with your pelvis, open the distance between yourself and the chair over 12 counts, keeping contact until the twelfth count.

Counts also give power to your stage management team for recording choreography. If actors start messing around with the lengths of the kisses that you choreographed, the stage manager can say "that was supposed to be a six-count kiss, and it turned into a 12-count kiss. Let's make sure that's a six-count kiss in the future." The counts can be used for any stage movement, not just intimacy. Rather than write that they cross left, stage management can write that they cross left over an eight-count.

Speed can feel subjective from actor to actor, so direction can be more effective if you can quantify the timing. If an actor does something too quickly, I say, "you're doing that cross over a five-count right now. Could you try it over an eight-count?" You can also ask the actor to describe their own movement in counts to get a better sense of their internal clock.

Sometimes it is helpful to count aloud to your own internal metronome to give the actors a clearer idea of the way you are thinking about tempo and counts. Usually, actors intuitively understand the counts and adjust their movements accordingly.

THE SHAPES

Most moments of intimacy and the physical gestures that happen during intimacy can be described by using one of three Shapes: Arcs, Angles, and Figure Eights.

The Shapes can be used to describe movements in a variety of applications. The most basic movement to apply shape to is a cross, or close. If you close the distance between yourself and an object across the room from you on an Arc, if you traced the path you traveled over the floor with your path to them will be curved. Similarly, an actor could open and close the distance between their pelvis and their partner's pelvis on an Angle (or line) or on an Arc.

Shapes can also describe the shapes that contact makes on the body. If the touch is dynamic, describe the shape of the path. For example, they could trace Figure Eights on their partner's back as a comforting gesture, or they could make dynamic muscle level contact with their fingers and palms on their partner's shoulders on an Arc.

Arcs (or Curves)

The first Shape is an Arc. An Arc is a curve, so if a gesture is curved or has some swoop to it, you might describe it as an arc. For example, a gesture where Partner A brushes Partner B's hair behind their ear with a skin-level touch over a four-count might be an arced gesture or a gesture that has a curve.

Angles (or Lines)

Our second shape is an Angle. Angles are lines that change direction in more of a zig-zag than a swoop. An angular gesture might be brushing something quickly off someone's shoulder or you might push someone away in more of an angular or linear gesture. A direct cross would be on an angle. Rapid opening and closing of distance between the front of one pelvis and the back of another might be angular.

Figure Eights

And then our third shape is a Figure Eight. These are particularly useful for finding motion in the torso or in the pelvis. For example, if Partner A is on top of Partner B and they are simulating intercourse, having Partner A find a Figure Eight in their tail while they open distance between their chin and their chest and make skin-level contact with the top of their torso and their neck tells a very different story than having Partner A make angular movements with their tail while making muscle-level contact with their torso and bringing their chin to their chest or to their shoulder.

Putting It on Its Feet

Try this in your space.

- Using a piece of furniture or a section of wall, close the Distance between yourself and the wall over a five-count. When you get there, with your hand, or your shoulder, or your hip, trace a curved or arced shape over an eight-count. Then open distance over a four-count.

- Now close the distance with the wall over a five-count and make linear or angular shapes with your hand, your hip, your shoulder. See how that story is different than the curved version. Open the distance with the wall.
- Now close the distance with the wall and, using your hand, your shoulder, your hip, over an eight-count, using muscle-level contact, find some Figure Eights and open the distance over a four-count.

By changing the shape of a contact, the general feel of the moment shifts. Having Partner A close the distance between the front of their pelvis and the back of Partner B's pelvis on a curve is very different than having them close that distance over an Angle, which is again different than having them close that distance and make a Figure Eight.

DESTINATION

Contact has to go somewhere. Whether it's a kiss, a touch, or where to look, be specific about Destinations. It's a simple thing that becomes very important when you are talking about bringing people's pelvises very close together.

Where does the touch go? Whether it's a kiss, a touch, or the look, you need to be specific about the Destination. The Destination is important because it provides

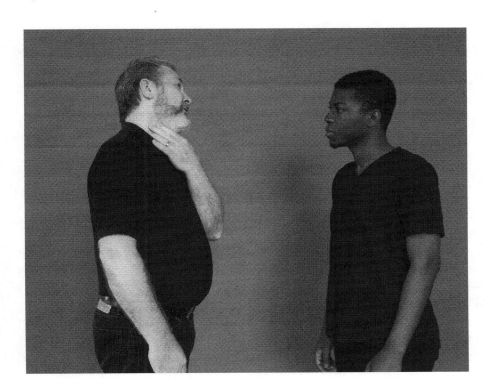

a specificity to a gesture that is recordable. The destination of a kiss could be my partner's lips. I can also have a starting destination and an ending destination. If I have a trail of kisses on my partner, I may have my starting destination being just above their hip, and then I have five points along the way that are the intermediary destinations before I arrive at the final destination on their opposite shoulder.

By using destinations we can chart the path of a gesture, determine where a gesture is landing, or where the intended gesture is to land. For example, if Partner A goes in for a kiss and Partner B avoids the kiss, the destination of Partner A's kiss may have been Partner B's lips but Partner B removes the destination.

We use destination, not target, because target implies a final destination of a gesture, rather than a journey to get there. Destination is useful when the real life destination of an intimate gesture is different than the simulated destination of that gesture. For example, later on when we talk through the process for staging a digital stimulation, in real life the destination of that actual intimacy would be a partner's genitals. In theatrical intimacy the destination of that gesture may be the upper inside back of the partner's thigh.

Because the destinations may differ from real life, it's incredibly important to specify them. Destination is also valuable because it eliminates the "where are you comfortable with?" conversation. If you have already established clear boundaries and reinforced them with Fences, then the actor's know where they have permission to touch. Comfortable becomes a less objective way to have a conversation about boundaries. Partner A can ask Partner B for four destinations for muscle-level contact. Then Partner A can move from destination one, to two, to three, to four without having to stop between each one and check in, because Partner B gave them permission for those touches. They can say Button at any time and it allows for things to move more quickly.

Destination can get actors from point A to point B to point C in space, but it's also useful when actors stray from choreography. If the destination has been specifically choreographed rather than saying, "Hey, stop grabbing my butt," or, "Don't touch my butt," you can remind the actor that the destination of the touch is their partner's lower back, rather than the back of their partner's pelvis.

EYE CONTACT

Eye Contact choices allow us into the mind of the character and help us understand relationships on stage. Most of the time, Eye Contact doesn't need to be choreographed. Actors will naturally find when to seek and when to avoid Eye Contact, but if there is a magical moment and you want to write it down, it can be useful to have Eye Contact as something that you are tracking. For situations with heightened emotion, like a story of sexual assault or seduction, setting the Eye Contact can be helpful for establishing and preserving storytelling.

The two options for eye contact are Seeking and Avoiding. Any combination of seeking and avoiding eye contact can tell any number of stories, depending on the context of the scene, and the relationship between the characters.

If two characters are closing distance with each other and seeking eye contact, that tells a very different story than if Partner A is closing the distance, Partner B is opening the distance, Partner A is seeking eye contact, and Partner B is avoiding eye contact. Different stories come from both partners seeking, or both avoiding, or closing distance while avoiding and seeking at the moment of contact.

Try using eye contact directions to score uncomfortable situations. If one partner is seeking and one is avoiding, you can start to stage an uncomfortable chase, or even a stalk, without needing to engage in the psychological language with the performers.

Try It with a Partner

Bring your hands up in front of you and have your partner do the same. Close and open distance between your palms, but play with variations on seeking and avoiding eye contact. Try some of these combinations to see how eye contact changes the story telling:

- Seek eye contact while you mutually close distance. Avoid the moment your palms touch.
- With your palms touching, one partner seeks and the other avoids. Open the distance on five counts as you switch eye contact seeking and avoiding.
- With your palms touching at skin level contact, deepen the touch to a muscle or bone level while you seek eye contact. Open distance on a one count and one partner avoids eye contact.

Other Applications

Eye Contact usually means seeking eye contact with someone else's eyes, but the versatility of this Ingredient is it can be used to direct gaze to other destinations. Use seeking eye contact as a way to replace "staring" or "ogling." "Check out their backside" becomes "seek eye contact with the back of their pelvis." "Stare at their breasts" can be replaced with seeking eye contact with their upper chest. "Don't get caught ogling them" can be "seek eye contact and avoid when you are noticed."

Instead of directing the character's emotional state, i.e. "you're nervous and don't know what you're doing," you can ask an actor to avoid eye contact with the part of their partner's body that they are making contact with.

VISIBLE POWER SHIFTS

Visible Power Shifts are often about who is on top of who and when that changes. Sometimes the power shift is more subtle (think a lean in a kiss) but taking and giving power in choreography creates dynamic intimate storytelling. Visible Power Shifts can be thought of as "giving the lead" to the other actor or putting them into the position of focus.

By saying Visible Power Shift, we're asking the actors to visually change the relationship between their bodies in space. The shift needs to be *visible*, not just

THE INGREDIENTS 53

54 THE INGREDIENTS

psychological, so there needs to be some kind of physical shift, not just an attitudinal one. The purpose of any movement on stage is to tell the story, so the position matters much less than what it communicates. There is no story that "doggie style" communicates that can't be communicated another way with desexualized language.

There are well-known names for many positions that one might engage within an intimate scenario. While it may be clear to you that a certain scene calls for X or Y or Z position, it can feel objectifying to be told to "get into X position." It may trigger loaded memories and real-world associations. It also runs the risks of overstepping carefully established boundaries. Asking for positions sexualizes the language and sexualizes the actors. Talking about power shifts helps keep the boundaries clear and gives the actors agency in how they physically tell the story.

As an added bonus, eliminating the position conversation also spares everyone the potential awkwardness of having (or not having) a developed personal sexual vocabulary. If you name a position your cast has never heard of, that may be an insight into your personal life (or at least your personal knowledge base) that isn't productive to actually doing the work of staging intimacy.

When working this way, because the actors have already established boundaries with one another, they're able to respect those boundaries that they've established without you needing to remember or track those boundaries. If you want one actor to be in a more powerful position because they have more text in that section of the scene, you can ask them to take the power or ask their partner to give them the power. They will choose movements that work for their boundaries.

If you just ask for a position, not only are you using sexualized language in rehearsal, but you're also potentially asking the actors to cross their partner's boundaries by putting themselves in positions that they haven't agreed upon. In asking for a Visible Power Shift you're allowing the actors to negotiate their own boundaries with their partner, rather than assuming an actors boundaries would allow for a particular position to work.

A sexual position might not cross a touch boundary, but it may make a demand of an actor's body that causes them physical discomfort. For example, if the director asked for a position that would require an actor with bad knees to kneel, and they tell the director they can't do it, everything stops while they brainstorm other positions. Or, they might try it and it looks awkward for them to move into that position because that isn't how their body naturally moves. If the director asks the actor to give their partner the power with a Visible Power Shift, they can choose a way of moving that accommodates their physical needs as well as their boundaries.

56   THE INGREDIENTS

> *Try Visible Power Shifts*
>
> Place your hands out in front of you with your palms about an inch apart and your fingers pointed forward.
>
> - Have your right hand take the power and move into a visibly more powerful position than your left.
> - Now have your left hand take the power.
> - Have your right hand give the power to your left hand. How is that different?
> - Try taking the power over a one count.
> - Use muscle level contact to give power.
> - Use muscle level contact to take power.
> - Take the power as you close the distance.
> - Take the power as you open the distance.

Add heavier and lighter levels of touch, increase and decrease the counts. Play with eye contact and shape. Try Visible Power Shifts on an arc or an angle.

Visible Power Shifts aren't always big and they aren't always about changing position. Sometimes, even the simplest intimate scenes need more movement. A classic couch make-out scene that shows up in the script at the end of a date that went well, could become stiff if the actors are just seated next to each other while they're kissing. Even if they're using lots of levels of touch and physical contact, and they're finding interesting gestures with each other, they may not get the variation that you're looking for. This is especially true if the make out scene needs to go on for a long time because of the demands of the text or because of other action happening onstage.

When a scene needs more movement, consider what you need from the physical storytelling. Are you signalling that the passion has overwhelmed the characters? Does it just need to be steamy? Do you just need a change visually? Do they need to move to the couch for the next bit of dialogue? Instead of telling them to jump into X position, ask for a Visible Power Shift to help them find their way into the next moment.

Using What Ifs and Visible Power Shifts

When coaching actors with Visible Power Shifts, it can be helpful to prompt them with What Ifs instead of taking time to introduce the ingredient out of context.

- What if you wanted to show that you were taking the power in this moment?

- What if you wanted to show that you are giving them the power?

- What if you showed them that you are equally powerful here?

- What if you take the power as you lead the move to the couch?

THE INGREDIENTS **57**

- What if you try to take the power and your partner takes the power instead?

- What if you try to take the power and nothing happens?

- What if the Visible Power Shifts takes you onto the bed?

BREATH AND SOUND

Making intimate sounds can be embarrassing. Actors are often nervous or self-conscious about making sound or even bold choices about breath. They might be afraid of making sounds that sound like moaning, or they'll make sounds that sound like their theatricalized version of moaning, which may not tell the story you're looking for at all.

One of the things you can do as a director or choreographer to support the choices that they're making physically is to offer some structure to support what they do vocally and with breath. Breaths and Sounds can be short, long, shallow, deep, high, low, or sharp. They can have the shapes of vowels or consonants. Describing Breath and Sound can also be used to avoid sexualizing the sound or breath of an intimate moment in a scene. By asking for long, low, "oh" sounds with short, sharp inhales, you can avoid asking for something with a sexual connotation like a moan with gasps of pleasure.

Short and Long

Short and long work much as you would expect and function similarly for both Breath and Sound. Use Counts as needed to define length.

- Try a five count inhale and a one count exhale.
- Flip the counts and add an "Ah" sound. One count in, five counts out on "ah".

Shallow and Deep

For breaths, this refers to the volume of air moving into the body. But for sound, shallow is more like unvoiced or partially voiced and deep is fully voiced.

- Try a long, shallow breath followed by a short shallow sound.
- Now try a short, deep breath followed by a long, deep sound.

High and Low

High and low sound refers to pitch, but high and low breath refers to placement. A high breath is in the upper chest while a low breath drops into the lower abdomen.

- Take a low, shallow breath. Exhale a long, low, shallow sound.
- Take a high, shallow breath. Exhale a long, high, shallow sound.

(Continued)

Sharp

Sharp adds another dimension to short breaths or sounds.

- Try a sharp breath.
- Try repeated sharp sounds.

Vowels and Consonants

Lots of intimate sounds are vowel sounds, but don't be afraid to use consonant sounds creatively. A long, low breath on an "s" or a short shallow "v" sound can provide a much richer texture than a wall of vowels.

Play with patterns of Breath and Sound and mix consonants in with the vowels.

Putting Voice, Breath, and Movement Together

Mixing sounds and movements together to tell different stories can have a sexy effect or a very comedic one.

For example if Partner A makes muscle-level contact with the front of their partner's body, making figure eights over a 12-count while they close the distance between their nose and their partner's neck, and their partner responds with short, sharp, low "ah" sounds, that can be comedic.

Quick movements such as closing the distance between the back of one partner's pelvis and the front of another partner's pelvis, repeated over one-counts with muscle-level touch, coupled with long, low "oh" sounds tells a different story.

More experienced actors or actors that are more comfortable or confident in their craft will probably make vocal choices on their own. Breath and Sound notation can then be used to record what works for the story.

Long, shallow, vowels, and consonants: all of these variations of Breath and Sound are meant to be prompts to the actor and give you language with which to record the sound the way you record the movement elements of the intimacy. Consider mixing Breath and Sound into text in ways that interrupt it and expand it.

GRAVITY AND WEIGHT

Gravity and Weight are valuable tools for fine-tuning intimate moments. They are little shifts that can make a big difference. This Ingredient is helpful particularly when actors get caught in the trap of trying to "act sexy". Oftentimes, that manifests as actor's pulling their weight off center. When weight shifts off to the side, it can look like stereotypical sexiness. But it may not be the story you are trying to tell.

THE INGREDIENTS   **59**

If an actor is light on their feet in a moment where you'd like them to be more powerful, or they are tentative about sharing body weight (leaning or laying on their partner), or they are concerned about squishing their partner, it can help to direct them specifically to imagine that their body is subject to increased gravity. Prompt actors to increase the effect of gravity in their pelvis or increase their partner's gravity as they lower their partner to the floor.

If Partner A throws their arm around Partner B's shoulder in a way that looks too aggressive, ask them to imagine that they have less gravity in their elbow and in their wrist, as it comes down over Partner B's shoulder. To make it look more aggressive, ask them to increase the effect of gravity. If Partner A is straddling Partner B because they've gone through a power shift and arrived in that position, and Partner A looks tentative, ask Partner A to increase the gravity between their belly button and the surface that Partner B is laying on to close the distance between their torsos.

Shifting weight to the center of the pelvis and increasing gravity can help an actor look more grounded. If an actor increases their gravity while they're on top of and straddling a partner, that's going to change the rhythm with which they open and close the distance with their partner.

Gravity and Weight can also make visible power shifts less awkward. Sometimes if everyone is attempting to manage their own body weight, the movement can become about logistics, rather than about the power shift. Have the partner taking the power be responsible for managing more of the weight in a shift and see how it smooths things out.

Playing with Gravity

Playing with Gravity and Weight is easy to try on your own.

- Imagine that gravity is having a more powerful effect on your pelvis. Let it pull you down, but just in your pelvis.
- Imagine it has a decreased effect on your sternum. Feel that float. Combine it with the increased pelvis gravity.
- Resting your hand on a tabletop, increase the gravity in your wrist and elbow and decrease the gravity in your fingertips

Playing with Weight

- Shift your weight to the left.
- Shift your weight back.

(Continued)

60 THE INGREDIENTS

- Share weight with the wall.
- Share weight with your chest and a doorframe.

Combinations with Gravity and Weight

- Shift your weight back and decrease the gravity in your pelvis.
- Share weight with a wall and increase gravity in your chest.
- Shift weight forward and increase gravity in your feet. Travel forward.

KISSING

They kiss. It's just a kiss. How hard can it be? Their heads come together and then they, well, kiss. But for how long? How hard? What does it look like? What do they do with their hands? Should they make noise? What about their feet? Where do noses go during kissing? What does the kiss mean? Tongue or no tongue?

The final Ingredient that we're going to take a look at is Kissing. Kissing is one of the most common elements in theatrical intimacy, and it's often one that's overlooked in regards to whether or not it needs to be choreographed. Many actors have been in a rehearsal where an actor is directed to "just kiss" another actor. That "just kiss" approach doesn't allow for establishment of boundaries. It doesn't allow actors to have a conversation about the purpose of the kiss, what the kiss is supposed to accomplish for the characters, how long the kiss should last, or at what level of touch the kiss should be happening.

Here are some best practices for integrating this final Ingredient.

Ground Rules

The standard for kissing in theatre is closed mouth, no tongue. There are very few situations in which an open mouth kiss would be necessary. In film, there might be a more legitimate need for a shot that would involve more open mouth kissing, potentially even with tongue. In that case, discuss it with the actors, determine how many takes you are going to do, and double check that everyone is healthy. But even in small spaces, the best practice for theatrical kisses is closed mouth, no tongue.

No kissing of any kind if actors are sick. The physical health of the actors should be of high priority and is of a higher priority than doing a particular kiss on a particular day. If they infect each other, you're not going to get anything done.

THE INGREDIENTS   **61**

Talk about that Kiss

It doesn't need to be a long conversation. In fact, just having a quick 30-second conversation about the purpose of the kiss and the reason for the characters to be kissing can solve a lot of directorial storytelling issues before anyone's face is on anyone else's face.

The first time a kiss comes up in a scene there can be confusion. If a partner goes for the kiss are they being too forward? If an actor goes for a kiss and their partner wasn't ready for it, are they being difficult to work with? Do they think that they aren't into it? If I go for the kiss are they going to think I'm too into it? If an actor is kissing their partner are they kissing their partner or is their character kissing the other character?

There's a lot of awkwardness that can come into play, because unlike a stage punch, in a stage kiss you don't swing your lips at your partner and carefully miss. We need to be explicit about the setup for kisses. The reason why we want to be so explicit about the descriptors around the kisses is that kisses tend to shift and change as the production continues.

This kiss conversation should happen for kisses that aren't mouth-to-mouth. A kiss to the neck, or a kiss to the chest, or a kiss to the inner thigh needs clarity too.

A kiss that's initially established as a three-count kiss may turn into a one-count peck by the time the cast gets to the fourth week of the run. Or it may have become a 12-count kiss because the actors have decided that they like doing the kiss, they like the reaction they're getting from the audience. Both changes would change the story of the kiss. By being explicit in the conversation and the choreography, you can make sure that the story you want to tell is preserved.

Opening and Closing Distance

Who closes distance to start the kiss? Who opens it?

Which character initiates the kiss? With that kiss, are both partners closing distance, or is one partner closing distance as the other partner's trying to open distance? Decide clearly so that when the actors then attempt the kiss there's no confusion about who is moving in and who is moving away.

Counts

How long is the close? How long does the kiss go on for? How long is the open?

Using the Ingredient of counts, you can be specific. This is a five-count kiss, or this is a 20-count kiss. It's a four count kiss, then a one count open, then a ten count kiss.

Level of Touch

Is this a skin-level kiss? Is it more of a touch? Or is it a muscle-level kiss? Or is this a level 3 kiss with level 2 in the hands?

Destination

Often, "they kiss" means a kiss on the lips.

Kisses need a destination. If the kiss is on the lips, that's great. But if the kiss is elsewhere on the body, establish the destinations clearly before going for it.

Kisses can travel. Map the destinations for a series of multiple kisses by having the partners find those points with their hands first.

The Kiss Conversation

The conversation between partners might look like this:

We kiss in this scene because it's the romantic climax of the play and our characters have fallen in love with each other. The kiss lasts five counts at muscle-level touch. Partner A closes distance. Once Partner A closes distance, Partner B will wrap their arms around Partner A, making muscle and bone-level contact with their back where they've been given permission to touch today. Closed mouth no tongue. I'm not sick. You're not sick. This kiss is going to be on the lips. Let's try it with our hands.

Trying It with Your Hands

The final step before trying the kiss: do it with your hands. This is one of my favorite tools for staging kisses in rehearsal. Once you have had the conversation (opening and closing counts, level of touch, etc.) do the kiss with a Placeholder (remember, it's a high five). Use that gesture to do all of the things you want to do in the kiss: opening and closing, level of touch, eye contact, counts all happen between palms. As a bonus, you can actually talk through the recipe and do it at the same time while you are working palm to palm. It's considerably more difficult to count out loud when faces are on faces.

Once the actors have tried it with their hands and gotten all of the elements where you want them, ask them if they are up for doing the kiss today. If yes, remind them of the closed-mouth, no tongue practice. If no, keep doing the Placeholder! When they are ready to move to the kiss, they will know exactly what to do.

Common Fixes for Bad Kisses

Even if everyone involved in a kiss feels great about it, it might look weird. Here are some of the most common issues and how to resolve them:

- The kiss looks stiff and boring.

Add a nose shift! Switching the noses from one side to the other with a tiny open can give a lot of life to a stiff kiss. Couple it with a visible power shift and you have a much more dynamic kiss.

- They don't know what to do with their hands.

Give a specific direction. Try "make muscle level contact on your partners back and move your hands in curves. Make muscle level contact with your forearms as well."

- They look like they don't know how to kiss.

Try changing the level of touch of the kiss. Muscle level, longer kisses tend to settle in a little nicer than a two count, skin level kiss does. Also suggest closing the distance with the chin. Often, the actors will close distance for the kiss with

their lips and noses. Closing with the chin fixes the line and makes the kiss look more solid.

- It's ... just ... awkward.

Check the distance between their pelvises, chests, chins. Increase the level of touch and activate the hands with shape. Slow everything down by two or three counts. Have them share more weight and find a visible power shift.

Alternatives to Kisses

Sometimes actors don't want to, or shouldn't, kiss. The reasons vary from cultural practices to personal boundaries to cold sores. Here are some options if a kiss isn't in the cards.

- Go nose-to-nose or nose-to-cheek. This is a nice option for a "sweet" moment. With a little breath, closed eyes, and closing the distance with the rest of the body, you will forget that a kiss was even called for.

- Close distance with chins and then come forehead to forehead.

- Sustained eye contact, a small close of distance, and a small, high inhale with a long, shallow exhale does the trick.

THE INGREDIENTS   **65**

PUTTING THE INGREDIENTS TO WORK

There are several ways to bring this work into your process, and no one way is categorically better than any other. It is all about what works for you. Personally, my way of working as a choreographer often depends on the style of the director and the amount of time I have with the cast.

Remember that this vocabulary isn't just for directors and choreographers. Actors can use the Ingredients to describe what they want to try, or what they think a moment looks like, or to make adjustments with each other, even if the director they are working with doesn't have these tools. They can use the Ingredients for documenting choreography so it doesn't shift and change over the course of a run.

The options for implementing this work generally fall into three broad categories: choreographing, tweaking, and documenting.

Choreographing

Much as a dance choreographer might give the footwork first and then add the arms, you can layer in more and more complexity, tweaking as you go, until you have arrived at the finished movement. Choreography with Ingredients can be done on the fly, in the room, and in collaboration with the performers or it can be sketched out ahead of time in rehearsal preparations.

When first developing a familiarity with the vocabulary or this technique, it can be intimidating or awkward to try to bring it into rehearsal and use it improvisationally. If this way of working feels like speaking in a foreign language, you may want to plan the moments out ahead of rehearsal. Writing it out beforehand doesn't eliminate opportunity to find things in the room, but it can serve as a starting point and as a way of getting everyone on the same page. If you want a passionate makeout on the couch, you can see it in your head, map it out, and share your ideas with the cast after they have established boundaries so that they have a clear idea of what you are looking for.

Choreographing with the Ingredients can be extremely efficient. Efficiency is especially valuable in a process where time is particularly precious. Choreographing with Ingredients can be just as fast as "just kiss each other," but with ethical and narrative integrity.

The language isn't complicated, but sometimes, putting it together can feel challenging. Not every Ingredient is for every scene. You don't put your whole pantry in your pancakes.

Here's an example of applying Ingredients to choreograph a scene. Here are the given circumstances:

Character A and Character B are going to passionately (and somewhat awkwardly) make-out on a couch in a college apartment. They were supposed to be reviewing their engineering lab notes. Paper everywhere. Character A is the more awkward of the two, but initiates the contact after a lingering touch to the hand when they both reached for the same graphing calculator. The make-out is interrupted when Character C enters from the kitchen with the second graphing calculator.

(Continued)

Remember: when you use desexualized language to describe intimacy, you avoid describing sex acts to actors, but you gain an ability to direct the movement as specifically as you might like. If I ask two actors for a passionate embrace, I have almost no control over what they will choose to do. It might be too violent. Or maybe too one sided. Or just awkward. Instead, describe each piece of the physical storytelling to the actors.

- Close the distance between you and your partner over a three count.
- Find muscle level contact between your chests and skin level contact with your nose on their neck.
- Activate the hands at muscle and bone level in figure eights on their back. Breathe high. Seek eye contact.
- Close the distance between your hips a few inches at a time. One count movements.
- Open the distance slightly between your chests, and with skin level contact on the back of their head with a hand, open the distance between your heads and seek eye contact.
- Character A closes distance for a 12-count kiss, nose switches every one or two counts, hands active in arcs and angles on faces, in hair, and on backs, long low "m" sounds and sharp inhales. Lots of sharing power back and forth.
- Character C enters, coughs, and Character A and Character B open quickly over a one, avoid eye contact, and long exhale through the lips (horse noise lip trill).

This is a fairly simple recipe for this moment, but I wouldn't give them all of this at once. After Boundary Practice, I would start choreography with who closes distance, then add level of touch and shape. I'd then go back to the beginning and add breath, sound, and eye contact.

Every intimate scene can be broken down, desexualized, and directed with the Ingredients. When movement is described in concrete, desexualized terms, it can be easily written down, leaving the actors with a recipe that they can follow into tech week and beyond. By using the Ingredients, you will be able to successfully create repeatable moments of theatrical intimacy. With practice and actor imagination, those moments will be dynamic, raw, compelling, and beautiful.

Tweaking

Some directors don't want to map out every moment, step by step. They want to give the performers more opportunities to explore and work more freely. Ingredients are a language for adjusting and tweaking what your actors find in the room and it doesn't need to feel like you are limiting freedom or puppet-eering the actors.

While working with the actors, after they have established boundaries, the actors could find a lovely moment together that ends in an embrace. You look at the embrace and it's almost exactly what you would hope for. If you want it to look a little bit more passionate, or a little bit more tender, or a little bit more awkward, you can use the language of the Ingredients to shape or tweak the moment.

This way of working works particularly well for simple moments. Often, a moment of touch doesn't need a lot of special attention, but just needs a little push in the right direction.

Documenting

Regardless of how the intimacy is created, it needs to be documented and preserved. Everyone on the team, from the stage manager to the director, can use the Ingredients to document the specifics of the intimacy, so that the hard work doesn't get lost throughout the process.

Even before the intimacy is finalized, Ingredients can be used to document the process. As many artists know, something beautiful often happens spur of the moment in rehearsal. When you come back from a break, or three weeks later when you're going into tech and everyone's in costume, the magic of that moment, for some reason, is forgotten and gone forever.

The solution is good documentation. Rather than writing down "hug" or even "passionately hug," specific, Ingredient based documentation allows for total specificity that doesn't rely on an actor feeling (or faking) "passionate" for it to work. By having a specific physical score, the actor can re-create that moment that was so magical when they first found it or when it was choreographed.

WRITING RECIPES

The purpose of this book is not to make you a choreographer, but to give you the tools to choreograph the intimate moments that you need to tell the stories you are trying to tell.

If you are going to try writing some Recipes outside of rehearsal, here are a few tips:

- Imagine it first. Try to see the way people move together in your imagination before breaking it down into Ingredients.

- You don't need to get all of the details right the first time. You don't even need to get most of them right. You can always tweak, add, and change on the next pass.

- Prioritize the Ingredients that are most visible for you. When you imagine this moment, do you see the level of touch? The opening and closing of distance? Start there, and add and build in complexity.

- Talk it out on your own. How would you explain what happens in the scene? Don't worry about using sexual language (because you are doing this outside of rehearsal). Translate the direction into Ingredients.

- When in doubt, play it out with your hands.

If you'd prefer to have the actors work the intimate moments out in rehearsal rather than choreographing them and writing Recipes ahead of time, the first step is to have the actors go through the Boundary Practice and clarify their Fences with one another.

Ask the actors, "What do you think happens here?" Encourage them to speak as their characters, not as themselves. "Catherine would do X," rather than "I'm doing X." You can ask them what they think their character would want to do in this moment, what their character's hoping to accomplish with the intimacy. You could also ask them questions in the language of the Ingredients. For example, who do you think closes the distance first? Who do you think opens distance? What level of touch do you think that distance is closed on? How quickly or slowly do you think that that happens?

By asking those questions, you can collaboratively discover the recipe with your cast, without just letting them improvise intimacy with each other. Improvisational intimacy is something to be avoided because it is often unproductive and can create a situation that feels unprofessional. Even if clear boundaries have been established, improvising intimacy, just like improvising a fight, isn't a safe choice.

This is a new vocabulary. Like learning a new language, fluency takes time and practice. Everyone starts somewhere, but when you start writing recipes, start with a kiss or a snuggle, not sustained simulated intercourse.

Notating and Coaching Choreography

I recommend making a table for notating this work because it prioritizes the most critical technical information that an actor would need in real time. If I told an actor to close distance, but didn't tell them how long to take, they would be left waiting. If I told them to use muscle level touch, but not where, they would be stuck.

The recommended order for prioritization is

1. Character
2. Counts
3. Actions (Open/Close, Eye Contact, Breath and Sound, Visible Power Shift, Kiss)
4. Destination
5. Descriptors (Level of Touch, Shape, Gravity and Weight)

For example, if the choreography is that Juliet is using her hands to close distance over four counts to make muscle level contact with her chest and Romeo's back, I would notate that in a table like this:

Character	Counts	Action	Destination	Descriptors
Juliet	Four	Close with hands	Chest to back	Muscle

If Romeo and Juliet both have choreography, it might look more like this:

Romeo				Juliet			
				Four	Close	Chest to back	Muscle
Two	Inhale	Low	Sharp		Seek eye		
Four	Close	Nose to nose		Four	Close	Nose to Nose	

(Continued)

70 THE INGREDIENTS

This helps keep the choreography organized, but it also helps me prompt actors as they are learning the movement. Side-coaching is very effective in this work because of how technical the language allows you to be. I often speak the choreography aloud so that the actors aren't struggling to remember complicated sequences, and I can use the language to perfect the choreography as they are working (seek that eye contact, shift to skin level, avoid eye contact on that open, etc.)

Actor Documentation

As the scene is being choreographed, the actors should be writing it down. It's important that the choreography gets recorded in the same desexualized language that it was choreographed in. This makes for a smoother process when things need to be tweaked or refreshed.

At the final dress rehearsal, when things are set, it is useful to have the actors each write out their choreography in their own words and bring it to the stage manager. This serves as an informal statement of understanding that the choreography is set and that there shouldn't be deviation.

Production Documentation

In addition to writing down the choreography, make an audio recording of the intimate choreography in rehearsal. Set up a voice recorder on your phone and talk through the beats of the scene as the actors go through it with their breath, sound, and lines. Count the counts and speak aloud what happens next. With an audio recording, the stage manager can confirm their own notation and use it as a reference for the future. Generally, video recordings of intimacy choreography in rehearsal should be avoided. A video of a simulated sexual act of context can create an unnecessary vulnerability.

Practicing with an Open Scene

Here is a short scene to get you started writing Recipes.

A: This is mine.
B: Oh, ok.
A: Thanks for tonight.
B: It was fun.
A: Yea. I had a good time.
B: Ok, so?
A: So?
B: Goodnight.
A: Goodnight

THE INGREDIENTS   71

Try writing Recipes for this scene to tell the following stories.

- End of first date that went well
- An awkward goodbye
- One character flirting and the other character noticing
- One character trying to escape
- Both characters trying to seduce each other

Practice will make you faster and more fluent in this new vocabulary and way of working, but it is also great practice in visualizing the physical storytelling in psychologically or emotionally loaded moments.

CHAPTER 3

Staging Intimacy

Theatrical intimacy refers to the whole spectrum of physical intimacy, including hugs, hand holding, kisses, and simulated intercourse.

Staging intimacy can be daunting and murky, but it doesn't need to be. Remember, theatrical intimacy is just storytelling, and we have already introduced the tools to cover the mechanics. Now, let's look at the other best practices, tools, and techniques for staging intimacy.

WHO IS IN THE ROOM

Before staging intimacy, decide who is going to be in the room. This is a decision that should be made with the actors involved in the intimacy. There are pros and cons to having extra people in the room, but it always comes down to what the actors prefer.

If the actors prefer to work without their castmates in the room, then ask everyone other than the actors involved in the intimacy and the stage management team to step out. If the actors interested in having their castmates in the room, invite the ensemble to stay. Some ensemble members may have a boundary about observing the choreography, so no one should be *required* to watch the process.

VULNERABILITY

Vulnerability, chemistry, or connection are elusive and can be tricky to establish between actors. Often, directors look for "chemistry" in auditions, with the hope that they won't need to tackle it later in the process. Sometimes actors take it into their own hands and try to fall a little bit in love with their partners.

This next technique is for practicing vulnerability, not creating chemistry, because we need to maintain separation between the truth of the characters and the reality of real life.

Chemistry is ambiguous. Vulnerability is a skill that can be taught and practiced. Vulnerability is setting aside, temporarily, the desire to protect oneself from emotional or physical harm. A common way for theatre practitioners to talk about vulnerability is being "open" or "available."

Thanks to evolution, our desires to protect ourselves in dangerous situations center around two major regions: our heads and our torsos. Something coming flying at you? You duck and cover your head. Projectile headed towards the center of your torso? You wrap your limbs around your soft center and turn to protect it. Our bodies naturally want to protect these precious, vulnerable regions. Many of us protect those vulnerable areas from emotional or social threats with our physical habits. We cross our arms, cross our legs, or take our bodies off center by sitting into our hips.

For the purposes of staging intimacy, we want to leave those vulnerable areas open to our partners. Agreeing, even just for the purpose of an exercise, to leave your center exposed and to take up space with your body can be scary. The energy that arises from that fear can make you more responsive to impulses, create connection, and may even result in emotional response. That's vulnerability. It may be exciting and uncomfortable as you start working on it.

Because we don't want to be actually afraid when we are on stage, we can practice standing in this vulnerable place, open and exposed, in training and rehearsal. We are training the body to embrace living in an open neutral position, bravely open to what the world has to offer. While you may have an emotional response to being physically open to a partner without any social mask or behavioral protections, all you need to do is just stand there. The sharp edges of fear and discomfort will fade as your body adjusts and being open and vulnerable will become as natural as stuffing your hands in your pockets.

Practicing Vulnerability

There are lots of ways to practice being open, available, and vulnerable. The first step is to practice vulnerability by yourself.

- Set a timer for five minutes.

- Stand or sit in an open, neutral position with soft ankles, knees, and hips.

- Allow your arms to fall to your sides.

- Choose a point on the imaginary horizon and breathe to it.

- Notice if you want to shift side to side or if you want to look away.

- At the end of the five minutes, notice what your body wants to do to cover or protect your center and get you out of that vulnerable state.

If you are an experienced actor, this is probably easy. But this straightforward exercise can be challenging for those newer to studying performance. You may have already outgrown the sting of vulnerability and stillness. With a group of first-timers, there is likely to be a chorus of giggling and shuffling as they negotiate social norms and try to get comfortable. Give them a minute to let that pass.

The longer they can embrace the openness of this position the more vulnerable they are to the audience. If they can bring this openness on stage with them, the audience will feel deeply connected to them.

If you are a teacher of performance, encourage actors to work on living in this position in everyday life. Standing in line at Starbucks, chatting with friends, washing dishes, folding laundry, or walking across town. Ask them to check in with their bodies throughout the day and make sure that they are keeping their centers open. The idea is to expose the head and center in non-threatening situations to acclimate to having them exposed during performance.

Partner Up

Being vulnerable by yourself is a lot easier than being vulnerable with a partner. As actors need to be vulnerable not only with a partner, but with a whole sea of people, they need to practice with a partner.

- Establish the Button.

- Go through the Boundary Practice and check in on Fences.

- With your partner, stand (or sit) about an arms length apart, facing each other in an open, neutral position with soft ankles, knees, and hips.

  ◦ Allow your arms to fall to your sides.

  ◦ Unclench your fists.

- Breathe through parted lips.

- Allow the talking and giggling to fall away.

- Look at their partner, open and vulnerable, and breathe.

  ◦ Don't stare through each other, but see your partner.

After the exercise, identify the impulses you felt to protect yourself and pull yourself off center. Remember that the desire to protect yourself is evolutionary, not a character flaw. It takes practice to set aside survival instincts.

Put It in Motion

Vulnerable, intimate moments rarely happens in static neutral, so let's introduce some movement.

- Repeat the set up for Partner Up.

- When you have found that open connection with your partner, step your right foot forward a foot length into a gentle lunge.

  ◦ If you are sitting bring your sit bones to the edge of the chair and allow your feet to stagger front and back underneath you.

- Staying upright, center open, imagine a giant exercise ball between you and your partner.
    - The gentle pressure between your center holds it off of the floor.
    - It has some give, but never deflates.
    - If it is helpful, support the sides of the ball with your hands to clarify the image and then allow your arms to drop to the side.
- Begin to pass the ball back and forth from your centers.
    - Work very slowly.
    - Resist the desire to pick up the pace. Speed is the enemy of vulnerability.
    - Keep the movement in the major muscle groups of your legs, rather than hinging from the pelvis.
- Work here for five minutes.

Like before, identify the impulses you felt to protect yourself. Recognizing habits is key to letting them go. If you can work and stay connected to your partner for five minutes, move on to the next step.

Introduce Touch

- Repeat set up for Partner Up.
- When you have found that open connection with your partner, step your right foot forward a foot length into a gentle lunge.
- Imagine the ball from Put it in Motion and shift it back and forth a few times.
- Ask your partner for permission to touch their palms.
  - Ask "May I touch your palms?"
  - Make sure you get a "yes" before you proceed.
  - If you don't get a yes, practice this exercise with a thick slice of air between your palms.

- Bring your palms to your partners.
  - Keep your elbows slightly bent.
  - Release your shoulders.
  - Use muscle level touch (share some weight/pressure with your partner through your palms).
  - Don't push your partner over.
- Shift the ball back and forth, maintaining this connection.
  - Make sure the shift is happening in the legs, not from hinging at the hips.
  - Make sure to keep your center upright and facing your partner.
- Feel the pressure of your partner's palms, give and take energy by exchanging weight.
  - Maintain eye contact and remember to breathe.
- Stay here for a few minutes, connecting and shifting back and forth, keeping your center open.
- Now, try giving and taking the energy more from one side of your body than the other.
  - Both partners give and taking energy at the same time.
    - For example, Partner A may be taking more on their right and giving more on their left.
    - If you don't have permission to touch your partner, you can do this with that thick slice of air.
  - Keep the center open even while your hands move forward and backward.
  - Stay grounded and keep shifting through your feet.
  - No leader or follower, just listening physically to your partner.
  - Continue to seek eye contact and breathe.

Moving Together

Now, let's practice moving this connection and vulnerability through space.

- Repeat set up for Partner Up.
- Keeping your center open, give and receive energy with steps forward and backward.

STAGING INTIMACY   79

- ◦ Maintain eye contact.
- ◦ Go slowly.
- ◦ Breathe.
- ◦ Keep that connection.
- Start to open and close the distance between you and your partner, by taking a few steps together or apart.
    - ◦ The ball between you is still there- it is growing and shrinking- continue to imagine holding it up.
- Play with different Distances.
- Introduce touch.
    - ◦ Remember the Button.
    - ◦ Be aware of your surroundings and remember your partner's boundaries.
        - ▪ If you don't have permission to touch your partner, work with that thick slice of air from the previous exercise.
    - ◦ Use touch to close distance.
    - ◦ Use touch to open distance.
    - ◦ Keep that ball between you.
    - ◦ Don't rush.

By the end of this step, the partners have established boundaries, been physically vulnerable together, moved together, exchanged energy, and explored opening and closing distance within their partner's boundaries. At this point, they would be well equipped to begin rehearsing an intimate scene.

STAGING SEXUAL VIOLENCE

Theatrical sexual violence is the consensual staging of a non-consensual story.

One of the most intimidating types of intimacy to stage is sexual violence. While the techniques are the same—boundaries, desexualized language, etc.—the inherently traumatic nature of the scenes, albeit imaginary, raises the stakes. Directors may be tempted to address this by opening up the rehearsal space to emotional processing and discussion of sexual trauma (their own and/or the trauma of the ensemble), but this is a mistake. Theatre is not therapy and directors and choreographers are not trained counselors, and you can do more harm than good by opening the door for a discussion of trauma.

Instead, lean even harder into the technique. Be especially sure to invest in desexualized language. Remind your cast early and often to practice self-care practices with De-Roling and the Button, so that they're not carrying the trauma of their characters out into their real lives.

Some combinations of Ingredients that are particularly helpful for staging sexual violence. If Partner A is closing distance while Partner B is opening distance, what we start to create is a chase. If Partner A in that same opening and closing score is seeking eye contact and Partner B is avoiding eye contact, we can start to create a narrative about power and pursuit without needing to say you're chasing and Partner B is trying to get away. That language, even though it's not directly related to the "intimate" contact of the scene, can be sexualized and triggering.

Begin with desexualized language during general blocking. Whereas in the scene that doesn't contain sexual violence, you might just ask the actor to back into a wall or to back into a door frame. If you're asking them to back into a wall or back into a door frame as part of a scene that contains sexual violence, you may want to consider using the desexualized language. Can you close the distance between your back and the door? Can you close the distance between your shoulder blades and that wall?

Take breaks early and often while staging sexual violence. A two or three minute break every half hour can give the actors a moment to breathe and check in with each other. Don't pressure the actors to tell you how they feel. Ask them if they have any questions about the choreography or if they want to review anything.

De-Roling in Sexual Violence

De-roling is especially critical here. If your actors are having a hard time, give them lots of breaks, but also facilitate de-roling to reaffirm that they aren't stuck their characters and that their relationship as colleagues is preserved, no matter how toxic the relationships of the characters might be.

STAGING NUDITY

"Nudity," in this context, means any level of dress (or undress) that is less than what an actor might wear to a rehearsal on any given day. Any nudity, from full nakedness to an actor removing a shirt, should be included in the casting call to ensure that the production hires an actor who will be comfortable with it.

During the first week of rehearsal, let the actors know what date(s) the nude scene(s) will be blocked and when you want them to start working at the show level of undress. Let them know the level of nudity needed to support the story and how it will happen (e.g., "you enter in a towel," "you take off your shirt," "you and your scene partner remove your clothing together"). In between blocking the scene and the day when the cast begins working in the nude, actors may work at any level of dress or undress they prefer. It's like setting an off book date, but for clothing.

Have the costume designer or dresser make sure robes are ready immediately offstage for actors who have nude scene, and ask if the actors want the robes handed

STAGING INTIMACY   **83**

to them or draped gently on them. More than once I have seen overly enthusiastic dressers startle the daylights out of an actor by flinging robes over them as if they were trapping wild animals.

The costume department may also be able to provide a pair of sweat pants and tee shirt dyed to match the actor's skin tone. This way, when the lighting designer sets the color levels, that actor doesn't need to be standing there naked for an extended period of time. Modesty pouches, tape, and pasties are all helpful for many types of nudity. Talk with your costume designer about how they can help you support the actors in this process.

With any intimacy on stage, it's important to have conversations with the entire production team regarding cell phone use during rehearsals, and this is particularly important in the case of nude scenes. If a show has nudity, consider banning phones except on breaks or when out of the room.

If there will be production photos of the nude scenes—and I argue that there should not be—include that in the casting notice as well. But there is very little reason for having a production photo of a naked actor—you're probably not going to use it in a mass mailing or in your portfolio. It may seem like a dramatic or vulnerable moment to take a picture of, and it is. But oftentimes the moment that would serve your portfolio best is the moment right before or right after the nudity. Help the photographer find those moments.

A common and well-meaning mistake that many directors make is to let the actors work up to the nude scene by asking them to rehearse in stages of undress (e.g., a bathing suit one week, topless the next, and fully naked the week after that). This attempts to ease the actors into it, but imposes a structure that might not fit— the actor may have different personal boundaries than the ones you imagine, or not be bothered at all and find the in-between stages a distracting nuisance. Giving them the option to dress as much or as little as they like between blocking and "off clothes day" puts the control back with the actor where it belongs. They might want to start working nude right away, or build up to it, or adjust to whatever mood they are in that day.

Have a Backup Plan

No director wants to hear that they may need to change a moment they are happy with, but sometimes there are more than just boundaries to contend with. Actors drop out and need to be replaced, or a big donor complains about the simulated sex and the artistic director says you need to change it. Not everything is within your control.

The good news is, you can control the result of an unexpected event by having a predetermined backup plan for moments of nudity. After you have staged the nudity, stage another version that serves the same storytelling purpose. The hope for a backup plan is that you never need it, but you always have it, and it is something that you had control over creating. Without a backup plan, your cast and crew might be left scrambling to solve the problem and they might lose track of the story.

Backup plan examples might include the following:

- The lights dim as the actor begins to remove their belt.

- The view of the partial nudity gets rotated upstage, so the audience can only see the clothed back of the actor.

- Add another layer (undergarments or an undershirt) so that the actors can remove a layer of costuming without being exposed.

Create the backup plan, rehearse it, tech it, and set it aside.

Additional Thoughts

- Telling an intimate, vulnerable, or violent story can be difficult, not only for the artists working on it, but also for audiences. Consider your audience (and the artists) and how a particular story might impact them. Just because you *can* stage graphic sexual violence or nudity doesn't mean you *should*.

- Sexual violence committed against (or committed by) members of marginalized groups can reinforce damaging social narratives that can contribute to real-world trauma and violence. This is often a season planning consideration, but check throughout the process of casting and staging as well. Storytelling is powerful, so be thoughtful in yours.

- Just as you would ask if you are the right person to direct a particular play, consider if you are the right person to stage a particular intimate narrative. Queer intimacy benefits from queer input as intimacy for disabled characters needs the perspective of disabled artists.

CHAPTER 4

Recipes

The Recipes that follow are for some common intimate scenarios. They are not meant to encompass all ways humans are intimate with each other, nor are they exhaustive in detail. They might not be exactly your taste, but you can adjust the flavors to your taste and to best suit the people you are working with. These are extremely basic Recipes and are in no way definitive stagings of any of these types of intimacy. When you introduce trans, non-binary, and queer sexualities and gender expressions into these Recipes, it opens up even more possibilities. Play with the Recipes. Mix them up and blend them. All of these Recipes are written for two partners, but additional partners can always be added.

Before using any of these Recipes, establish a Button, take the actors through the Boundary Practice, and introduce them to the Ingredients that require introduction. Make sure you are doing your best to maintain a desexualized rehearsal environment and document what you come up with.

The Recipes are outlines for how to assemble individual Ingredients into intimacy choreography. The Recipes listed, like cooking recipes in life, are meant to be riffed off of, modified, and fused together to suit the unique tastes, or needs of a particular production.

In the Recipes that follow, the steps are written out as a little narrative to assist your understanding of the images being created. Practice the notation for each variation of the recipe that follows by writing your own version of the recommended prioritization of information.

Embrace

Basic Ingredients

- Opening and Closing Distance
- Counts
- Level of Touch
- Eye Contact

(Continued)

Optional Ingredients

- Shapes
- Breath and Sound
- Visible Power Shifts
- Gravity and Weight

Embrace Recipe

1. Partner A and Partner B start a few feet apart.
2. Partner A and Partner B close distance over three counts for a muscle level contact with the full front of their body, using their arms to close the distance and finding muscle level contact on their partner's back. Sustain for three counts.
3. Partner A and Partner B open distance over three counts.

RECIPES **87**

Variations

One Sided Embrace

1. Partner A and Partner B start a few feet apart.
2. Partner A Closes Distance over two counts to make muscle level contact with Partner B's body using their arms to close the distance. Sustain for five counts.
3. (Optional: Add long, high inhale through the nose for Partner A.)
4. Partner B opens distance using skin level touch over four counts, avoiding eye contact.

Welcome Home Embrace

1. Partner A and Partner B start far apart.
2. Partner A and Partner B seek eye contact.
3. Partner A and Partner B take short low breath.
4. Close distance over two counts to make bone level contact with their arms and the fronts of their bodies, using their arms to close the distance. Arcs in the hands. Sustain for five counts.
5. Partner A and Partner B make small visible power shifts back and forth.
6. Partner A opens distance over one count to seek eye contact, making skin level contact with the face.
7. Close distance for two count bone level full-body contact.

Kiss

Basic Ingredients

- Opening and Closing Distance
- Counts
- Level of Touch
- Eye Contact
- Kiss

Optional Ingredients

- Shapes
- Breath and Sound
- Visible Power Shifts
- Gravity and Weight

Kiss Recipe

1. Partner A and Partner B seek eye contact.
2. Using their hands, Partner A and Partner B close distance with their noses and chests.

(Continued)

3. Two count, muscle level kiss.
4. Two count open distance.

Variations

First Kiss

1. Partner A and Partner B avoid eye contact.
2. Partner A seeks eye contact, Partner B catches them.
3. Partner A closes half of the distance over three counts.
4. Partner B closes half of the distance over two counts.
5. Two count skin level kiss.
6. Three count open distance.

Making Out

1. Partner A and Partner B seek eye contact.
2. Using their hands, Partner A and Partner B close distance with their noses, pelvises and chests.
3. Ten Count, muscle level kiss. During that ten counts, add a mix of:
   - Muscle and bone level shapes
   - Short exhales through the nose
   - Small visible power shifts
   - Big visible power shifts
   - Sharing weight and taking it away
4. Three count open distance.

Oral Sex

(*Continued*)

90 RECIPES

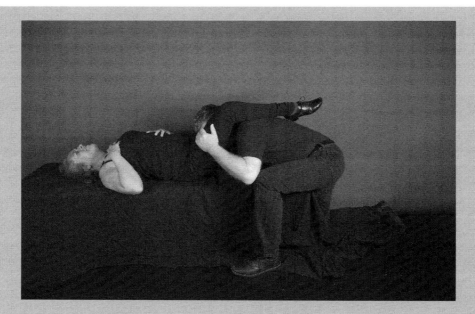

Basic Ingredients

- Opening and Closing Distance
- Counts
- Level of Touch
- Shapes
- Breath and Sound
- Kiss

Optional Ingredients

- Eye Contact
- Visible Power Shifts
- Gravity and Weight

Internal Sex Organs

1. Kiss inside of thigh, muscle level, two counts.
2. Close distance between nose and opposite upper inner thigh.
3. Muscle and bone level contact with the hands on the outside of Partner A's thighs.
4. Make slow skin and muscle level figure eights and arcs with nose on the upper inner thigh.

External Sex Organs

1. Kiss down chest, muscle level, two counts.
2. Close distance with nose and top of thigh.

RECIPES 91

3. Close distance with chin and opposite thigh.
4. On an arc, close and open distance with the nose on a path between the belly button and top of thigh.

Recipient Response Options

- Open distance between chin and sternum.
- Seek eye contact.
- Draw arc with nose in space above you over an eight count.
- Long slow inhale on "s".
- Short exhale on "f".
- Short, deep breaths.
- "M" sounds.
- Muscle level contact with Partner A's head/hair.
- Dynamic movement in hands and feet.

Masturbation and/or Digital Stimulation

(Continued)

92 RECIPES

Basic Ingredients

- Opening and Closing Distance
- Counts
- Level of Touch
- Shapes
- Breath and Sound
- Kiss

Optional Ingredients

- Eye Contact
- Visible Power Shifts
- Gravity and Weight

Internal Sex Organs

1. Bring fingers to inside of thigh, muscle level, two counts.
2. Close distance between fingers and opposite thigh.

RECIPES   **93**

3. Make skin and muscle level figure eights and arcs on upper thigh with fingers, keeping wrist close to pelvis.
4. Open distance between wrist and pelvis and draw arcs on opposite thigh with thumb, palm up.
5. Bring wrist to front of pelvis or opposite thigh and using skin level contact open distance between wrist and pelvis, moving towards belly button.

External Sex Organs

1. Fingers move down chest, muscle level, eight counts
2. Close distance with palm and top inside of thigh.
3. Keeping contact with the fingertips to the inside of the thigh, rotate the wrist on an arc with muscle level contact.
4. With the same hand, switch thighs. Make contact with the top inside of the thigh (hip crease).
5. Close and open distance the palm of the hand on a path between the belly button and top of thigh with muscle level contact, gently closing hand while moving upward and opening it while moving downward.

Recipient Response

- Open distance between chin and sternum.
- Draw arc with nose in space above you over an eight count.
- Make muscle level contact with working hand.
- Long slow inhale on "s".
- Short exhale on "f".
- Short, deep breaths.
- "M" sounds.
- Dynamic movement in hands and feet.

Penetrative Sex

Basic Ingredients

- Opening and Closing Distance
- Counts
- Level of Touch
- Eye Contact
- Kiss

Optional Ingredients

- Shapes
- Breath and Sound
- Visible Power Shifts
- Gravity and Weight

(Continued)

94 RECIPES

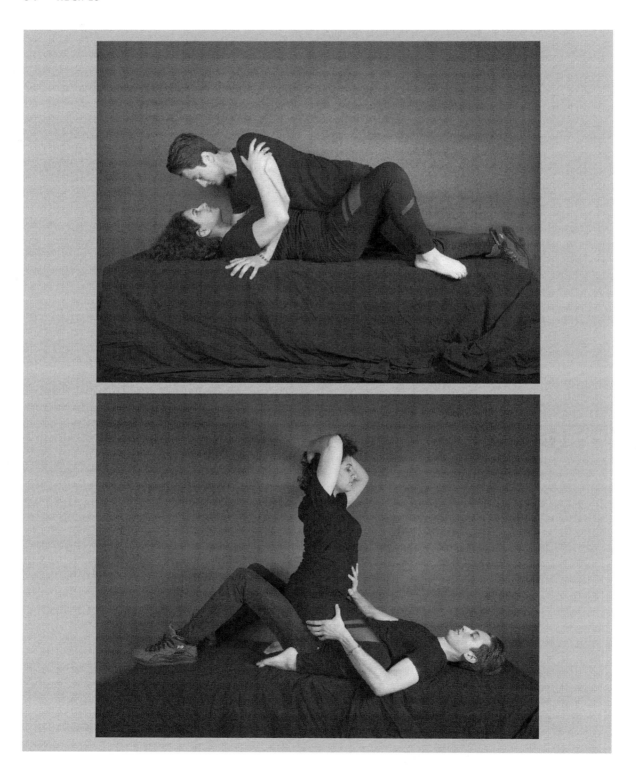

Recipe

1. Partner A opens distance between knees slightly.
2. Partner B closes and opens distance with their upper inner thigh crossing their partner's center line to the opposite upper inner thigh. Muscle level contact.

   a. If Partner A is on their back, Partner B would bring their right upper inner thigh to Partner A's upper inner thigh.
   b. If Partner B is on their hands and knees, Partner B would close the Distance between their right upper inner thigh to Partner A's left upper inner thigh.

Variations

- Bottom of the glute or upper inner rear thigh is the destination, cross the center line on and arc or curve.
- Shift Destination to front or back of pelvis, top of one thigh (Partner A in more powerful position). Knees to inside and outside of Partner B's thigh.
- Add visible power shifts, change tempo, vary levels of touch.
- Change shape of opening and closing.
- Add kisses to the mouth and body.
- Pull bed coverings and set dressing between bodies to modify destinations further. If the level of dress and the boundaries of the actors would bring genitals close together, modify the choreography or add padding and shields. Work with your costume designer so that they can support you and the actors in the process.

Feeling and Touching

Basic Ingredients

- Opening and Closing Distance
- Counts
- Level of Touch
- Shapes

Optional Ingredients

- Eye Contact
- Visible Power Shifts

General Recipe

- Choose counts
- Choose level of touch

(Continued)

Under Clothes

- Clarify fences for skin to skin contact if contact is under clothing.
- See Masturbation and/or Digital Stimulation recipe.
- Play with counts and extending destinations onto thighs and torso.

Teasing

The tease can be more important to the story than contact. How a character teases depends heavily on the context in the scene, but here are some ideas to get you started.

- Partner A closes distance over 12 counts on a curve. With fingertips, make a slow, skin level, figure eight on their torso and around the back of their neck.
- Avoid eye contact as you make contact with Partner A's hands to Partner B's knees. Seek Eye Contact. Avoiding Eye Contact and maintaining physical contact, move palms to upper inside of Partner B's thighs.

- Removing clothing. Do it slowly and drop it like gravity has no effect on it.
- Increase gravity in back of body (shoulder blades and back of pelvis). Let that weight bring you gently to your knees over six counts. Close distance with Partner B on hands and knees. Maintain increased gravity as the crawling partner travels.

Removing Clothes

Removing clothes takes a lot of forms from just tossing off a partner's jacket to a more elaborate stripping. All clothing removal should be rehearsed with rehearsal garments and put on the rehearsal schedule.

Ingredients to play with:

- Counts
  - Can you remove Partner A's sweater over eight counts instead of three?
- Level of Touch
  - Try using a powder level touch to remove that.
- Eye Contact
  - Seeking or avoiding with other characters/audience.
  - Destination of eye contact. Seek eye contact with that jacket when you throw it.
- Destination
  - Pulling pants off from the ankles is very different than from the waist.
  - Is the intention of the clothing removal to seek Eye Contact or touch with a particular part of their partner's body?
- Shapes
  - Find more arcs and curves as you remove that garment.
- Breath and Sound
  - Can you find a sharp inhale as that garment drops?
- Gravity and Weight
  - Can you give those pants more weight as you pull them off of Partner B?
  - Try dropping it like they weigh nothing.

(Continued)

RECIPES

> ### *Intimacy with Lots of Text*
>
> Sometimes playwrights give us a lot to say and a lot to do. Working lines in between gasps and kisses can be tricky, but there are good options for when one or more people in an intimate scene need to speak and be understood.
>
> One partner with lines
>
> - Oral Stimulation from other partner(s)
> - Digital Stimulation
> - Masturbation
> - Feeling
> - Kisses on bodies
> - Intercourse simulation with speaking partner in more powerful position
>
> Multiple Partners with lines
>
> - Digital Stimulation
> - Feeling
> - Alternating body kisses
> - Visible Power Shifts (i.e.: on a couch)

STYLIZATION

Theatrical intimacy doesn't need to be realistic to be effective. Directors choose to stylize intimacy for many reasons. Whether it is for actor comfort, an aesthetic choice, an audience consideration, or a request from the company, approaching the intimacy in a stylized way can support the production in many of the same ways more realistic intimacy would.

Intimacy can be stylized in a number of ways. A simple option is to play with distance. If the story being told is of a caress down the length of Partner A's back, have Partner A stand five feet downstage of Partner B. Partner B makes the gesture, on an arc, from their position upstage and Partner A responds as if they are being touched.

Another option is to stylize with symbolic touch with another part of the body or with an object. Symbolic contact with another part of the body can tell the story of physical intimacy. While the intimate moment you might be creating the illusion of intercourse between Partner A and Partner B, you may find touching hands and collarbones with breath and sound to be enough. For the same scene, you could employ a set piece to stand in for Partner B, and have Partner A make contact with the arms of a chair as Partner B responds.

Many of the most elegant solutions involve design choices. A sound cue, a fade of the lights, or an additional layer of garments can help support a director's decision to stylize intimacy. Talk with the design team early on in the process about moments you are interested in staging non-realistically and see what the team can come up with.

CHAPTER 5

Production Logistics

Everyone involved in a production can contribute to a more consent-based, desexualized, professional process.

Every producing organization is unique, so consider which combinations of tools will best support your organization in concert with the tools and systems already in place.

COMPANY AND DEPARTMENT POLICIES

Theatre companies and departments should develop Intimacy, Nudity, and Touch policies to support consensual, safe practices at the institutional level. Policies should include definitions of theatrical intimacy, nudity, and sexual violence, casting policies, rehearsal and production documentation guidelines, and any best practices (desexualized language, Boundary Practice, etc.) that the theatre wants to adopt. Include behavioral expectations and what constitutes grounds for removal. Consult with any relevant unions to keep abreast of current policies.

Be sure to provide a copy of the policy to existing company members, new hires, and anyone working as a guest artist with the company.

CHAIN OF COMMUNICATION

The Chain of Communication is a document that outlines the best practices for communicating concerns in a process. It lists the name and contact information of all of the relevant parties. This should be included in any first-rehearsal handouts and should be posted near the sign-in sheet.

A Chain of Communication might include the Equity Deputy, Stage Manager, Production Stage Manager, Director, Artistic Director, and Board Members of a theatre. They should be listed in an order that makes it clear who should be contacted first, second, etc. If a member of a production is uncomfortable going to any person on the Chain, they should go one link higher until they find someone to bring their concerns to.

This same document can also include resources like a nearby counselling center, crisis hotlines, and general emergency numbers.

102 PRODUCTION LOGISTICS

If you are in academia, try to keep students out of the Chain of Communication. Power dynamics between peers can lead to students feeling overburdened. Include a faculty or staff member unrelated to the production in the Chain, as well as contact information for the Title IX office.

CASTING

Write audition announcements and character breakdowns that include all of the content that might be required of a particular role. For example, if you're doing a play that involves nudity and sexual violence, make that clear in your description of the show that you're casting, and then underneath the character descriptions include which of those things that character might be asked to do.

Here's a simple sample description:

The Play, by Playwright, is a story about June and Mary and their roadtrip across the country. This play involves choreographed physical intimacy and partial nudity.

June: 25–35. Outgoing, brilliant, and kind. This role involves choreographed physical intimacy.

Mary: 30–40. Passionate and funny. Always surprising June to make her laugh. This role involves choreographed physical intimacy and Mary appears in a bra and underwear for a long scene.

Descriptions like this are important for new, or lesser known, works because the actors wouldn't know what to expect. But don't leave the description out just because the play is popular, or even canonical. Don't leave it to chance that the actor you end up casting for Stanley hasn't read *A Streetcar Named Desire* and won't do scenes with sexual violence.

The second step is to introduce an Audition Disclosure Form. This is a form that you can develop (or use the example below) to ask actors what their comfort levels are with various intimate, violent, or content related moments.

Audition Disclosure Form

Please indicate your preferences for working on productions with the following material:

Theatrical Intimacy

Note: All theatrical intimacy will be choreographed.

	YES	NO	MORE INFORMATION NEEDED
Performing or witnessing realistic theatrical intimacy?			
Kissing?			

Performing or witnessing stylized theatrical intimacy?

Performing or witnessing simulated sexual assault?

Performing or witnessing stylized simulated sexual assault?

Performing or witnessing non-sexual physical contact with others?

Violence

Note: All violence will be choreographed.

	YES	NO	MORE INFORMATION NEEDED
Performing or witnessing simulated acts of violence?			
Performing or witnessing situations involving theatrical firearms?			
Performing or witnessing simulated self-harm?			

Nudity

	YES	NO	MORE INFORMATION NEEDED
Performing or witnessing partial nudity (including revealing costumes)?			
Performing or witnessing on-stage costume changes?			

Other Content

	YES	NO	MORE INFORMATION NEEDED
Performing or witnessing substance abuse?			
Performing or witnessing profanity?			
Performing or witnessing derogatory language?			

(Continued)

104 PRODUCTION LOGISTICS

> Performing or witnessing subject matter
> involving sexual assault?
> Performing or discussing actions related to
> disordered eating?
> _____
>
> Other comments:
>
> If you need to update your Audition Disclosure Form, please contact _____.

You can ask specifically about things that come up in your show or if you're casting for a season or a repertory company or doing general auditions, you can ask include a more comprehensive list of content. The Audition Disclosure Form is a separate form from the standard audition form, and it can be completed at the audition or any time prior.

After auditions, directors can review the Audition Disclosure Forms and check the potential call-back list against the disclosures to see if there is a conflict. If there is a conflict, the director can choose another actor or consider reconceptualizing the moment to make it work for the actor's boundaries. If an actor has selected that they need more information, that conversation can happen at or prior to call-backs.

This process creates opportunities for actors to state their boundaries and ask clarifying questions about the demands of a role. Out of a desire to be cast, actors may intentionally or unintentionally misrepresent their boundaries. There is no perfect system, and while the Audition Disclosure process isn't perfect, it creates the most opportunities for consent in casting.

Placeholders in Auditions

If the scene or side for an audition involves any physical intimacy or violence, have the person running the auditions instruct the actors to use a Placeholder for those moments. By using a Placeholder, actors can focus more on playing the scene and less on whether or not their scene partner is going to try and slip them tongue.

Recasting and Reimagining

If you have clearly stated in your casting announcement what's required of a role, and the actor has accepted that role, you are well within your rights to re-cast an actor who's unable to fulfill those obligations. Re-casting has a bad reputation but it is a tool that can support boundaries in creative processes.

"I appreciate your work on this role. As you know, this is required for this role, and it's important to me, and the production company, that we respect your boundaries. Because we need this moment, and that doesn't work for your boundaries, we are going to recast the role at this time. We appreciate you being a part of this process, and we look forward to finding an opportunity for us all to work together in the future."

A positive frame doesn't ensure a comfortable conversation, but it sets the actor up to work with the company again in a positive light. This framework is designed to respect the boundaries of the actor being recast. It does not apply to an actor being removed for bad behavior. If an actor is removed because they have been crossing boundaries, document the removal in the company records.

REHEARSAL SCHEDULES

Although they may be subject to change, mark the days for staging intimacy, nudity, and sexual violence on the schedule so that the actors know those dates in advance. Be in communication with the involved actors as the date gets closer to determine their preferences regarding who is in the room and about anything they might need (knee pads, robes, etc.).

INTIMACY CALLS

While a fight call is always necessary to rehearse the violence, an intimacy call is not. Intimacy call has a lot more in common with a dance call than a fight call. Intimacy calls should be run if the choreography goes awry, needs a brush up, is complicated, or if the actors request it. If there is a moment of violence in your intimate scene, consider running just that moment rather than running the full sequence.

Always budget time in the production process to run a call should the production need it, but it may not be necessary. If there is an intimacy call, the stage manager should run it.

INTIMACY CHOREOGRAPHERS

Do you need to hire an intimacy choreographer? This is a common and complicated question because the answer depends on the demands of the production and the skills of the people involved.

If the tools in this book have been successfully synthesized by a member of the production team and they are taking on the role of choreographing the intimacy, you might be good to go on your own. But if the intimacy is complicated, or the production team doesn't have sufficient time, energy, or brain space to dedicate to introducing this process, then bring in a pro. If you feel unsure, reach out to an intimacy choreographer or to Theatrical Intimacy Education and talk through your concerns.

If you decide to bring in an intimacy choreographer, here are some questions to ask to see if they will be a good fit for your processes:

(Continued)

- How do you establish boundaries? What is your technique for adapting to changing boundaries?

- What is your training? Who have you worked with? Do you have references?

- What are your best practices for staging intimacy?

- What does your process look like?

- How long do you think the intimacy choreography will take? How many rehearsals will you want? Over what timeframe?

- How do you handle notating, documenting, or recording choreography?

- If the director wants to make changes, what does that process look like?

This field is evolving, so I encourage you to regard certifications and fancy titles with a grain of salt. There isn't a standard for certification in the field, so do your homework before bringing someone onto your team. Seek out experienced intimacy choreographers who bring approaches that align with your values. Remember, there are lots of very qualified people out there who have been doing intimacy work without certifications for years. They might be a great fit for your process. There isn't anything wrong with a certification, but don't assume a certification is shorthand for "the right fit."

STAFFING THE PRODUCTION

Designers and technicians have boundaries, too. Communicate with the whole team to ensure that the right people sign on for the project.

- If the project involves nudity, intimacy, violence, or other potentially sensitive material, include that in your initial inquiries to designers and technicians along with the dates of the project and other relevant information. If you are staffing an entire season or shows in repertory, you may want to send out something similar to an audition disclosure so people can indicate their boundaries with a wide range of topics.

- Include play synopses in season announcements. Do that legwork for your team so that they're not accidentally signing on to projects that don't work for their boundaries.

- If someone is working on a project and discovers during the course of the project that they're having a hard time with the material, introduce them to de-roling or offer to shift their assignment on the project.

- Teach your production managers to use desexualized language in your process when you're talking about intimate scenes, and encourage designers to do that as well.

CONSIDERATIONS FOR DESIGNERS AND TECHNICIANS

The moments before a show are packed. Costumes and wigs and warm ups and fight calls and mic checks are all tightly scheduled to allow for maximum efficiency and the latest possible call time for all parties involved out of respect for everyone's time. That quest for efficiency can make common courtesy fall by the wayside.

All members of the production should follow the best practices of asking people before touching them and maintaining a desexualized working environment.

Lighting designers can play a large role in supporting the director's vision, but also in supporting the actor's boundaries in moments of intimacy or nudity. This support can range from softly lighting nudity from the sides to ensuring a full blackout when the intimacy choreography ends. Costume designers, costume technologists, and costume crews come into a lot of physical contact with performers. It's a requirement of the job. Here is a statement of costume-related best practices that may provide a useful template for clarifying those requirements and expectations:

When an actor is cast in a production, they should come to their scheduled fitting prepared to participate in the fitting process at that time.

Fittings involve:

- Removal of street clothes down to undergarments (Actors are responsible for wearing opaque, neutral-tone, full-coverage undergarments to all fittings)

- The fitting of garments close to the body

- Physical touch to adjust fit to designer specification

- Interaction, including physical touch, by various personnel including the draper, designer, and assistant designer

Actors and Shop Personnel have the following tools in a fitting:

- Saying "Button"

- Request two-minute break

- Request a reduction in the number of people in the room

- Request that the door be open or closed

- Request to be fitted in an open or closed area of the shop

- Request help or additional privacy for dressing or undressing

- Ask questions for clarification

The measuring process for costume fittings requires accuracy. This process involves physical contact with the measuring tape and minimal touch from the measurer. Actors and Shop Personnel have the same tools available during measurements as above.

Production management can play a role in ensuring that the casting notice includes all of the appropriate information and that the information is distributed not only to potential auditioners, but also to potential members of the production team. Production managers can also ensure that a Chain of Communication is created and is distributed at the first production meeting.

Projection designers should be thoughtful in their use of actors' bodies as projection surfaces and thoughtful about using images of actors bodies as projection content if that has not been disclosed in the casting breakdown, early on in the casting process, or developed in conversation with the actors.

If you're working with any props that come into physical contact with the actors, make sure that they are stored safely and that they're not around for actors to tamper with. Of course, actors shouldn't touch props that aren't theirs anyway, but when props like riding crops and handcuffs become a part of the landscape of a show, actors can sometimes forget their manners.

If there's more advanced physical intimacy in the production that involves any kind of simulated intercourse or digital or oral stimulation, consider having some additional padding or spacers available. These can be simple and made out of thick pieces of felt that can be added into costumes or built into set pieces that can be flipped up to create additional barriers between actors. The choreographer for the intimacy should be in conversation early on in the process with the costume and scenic designers to plan for additional cover.

FRONT OF HOUSE STAFF AND USHERS

When there is intimacy, nudity, or sexual violence in a production, consider implementing a zero-tolerance policy about cell phones or camera equipment in the space. Instruct ushers to remove patrons with their phones out or in use during the production to protect actor privacy.

CONTENT WARNINGS

Some theatres and directors resist the use of content warnings, fearing that it will somehow pull an audience out of the moment if they know what's coming. Audiences are surprisingly well practiced, however, in forgetting everything that's told to them outside of the theatre and jumping into the world of the play. The audience members that don't have boundaries that relate to the content warnings are going to forget about them almost immediately. The audience members that do have boundaries that relate to the content warnings can consent to watch the performance with an understanding that this production may encounter their boundaries.

Use content warnings for violence, sexual violence, incest, molestation, nudity or simulated sexual acts, and anything that an audience member might want to know about. A production may lose a few audience members over a content warning, but losing a few audience members for one show is far better than having an audience member traumatized by a performance and choosing never to return.

BOUNDARIES WITH THE AUDIENCE

Audience consent is critical. Notify your audience beforehand if there are interactive moments in the piece, and develop a mechanism so they can opt-in or out. Consider having an area of the audience that you designate as a participation zone, so that audience members can choose whether or not to sit in a participatory seat. Always be mindful about making physical contact with the audience. If the piece is interactive, the audience will need to be oriented to the rules regarding touch and consent for the production so that they can participate consensually.

Audience boundaries are particularly important in immersive and site specific work where the more standardized rules of the proscenium theatre aren't available and audiences aren't sure how to behave. Consider working with a consent specialist when constructing immersive or site specific work.

TALKBACKS

While one of the most common questions at a talk back is "How do you memorize all those lines?" When there's intimacy in the show, the questions "how did you stage that intimacy?" and "was the intimacy real?" come up. Feel free to share with your audience this process that you've engaged with. Lifting the curtain on the process of staging intimacy helps prevent audience members from thinking that the things that they watch actors go through are real. Misinformation about theatrical intimacy leads to a perpetuation of bad practices and also can inhibit the cultural shift around moving towards more consensual and desexualized staging of theatrical intimacy.

Audiences are often interested in seeing an abbreviated version of the Boundary Practice if there is a discussion of how consent played a role in the production process.

POST-SHOW REVIEWS

Not every company can regroup after closing night, but find a way to check in with the whole team about the processes and procedures used to support the intimacy, nudity, and sexual violence in the production. Some questions to consider for your discussions:

- How did our Intimacy, Nudity, and Sexual Violence policy serve the needs of the production?

- Were there any issues in the production?

  - If so, were they reported?

  - How were they handled?

  - What can be done better next time?

- How can we build on this process moving forward?

CHAPTER 6

Staging Sex: A–Z

Here are all of the steps of a sample process for a play that involves a moment of theatrical intimacy and a moment of nudity. In this example, the director casts the show, has chosen to stage both moments, and will be around for a post-process discussion.

- Select the play
- Create the audition notice. Include:
  - A short synopsis
  - Content warnings
  - Detailed descriptions of what is required of each character

- Hold Auditions. Use the following tools:
  - Audition Disclosure Form
  - Placeholders for any intimacy or violence
- Casting
  - Consult Audition Disclosure Forms
  - Discuss any actor concerns
- Prior to first rehearsal, the entire company receives
  - The Theatrical Intimacy, Nudity, and Sexual Violence Policy including behavior expectations
  - Rehearsal Schedule with Intimacy marked on it
- First Rehearsal
  - Use Open Questions
  - Discuss three big ideas
    - Consent (Make asking before touching a company rule)
    - Desexualized Language
    - All Intimacy will be choreographed
  - Introduce Button
  - Distribute Chain of Communication
  - Discuss timeline for Nudity with involved actors
  - Use Placeholders for intimate moment in the table read
- First Week
  - All actors learn Boundary Practice
- Choreography Rehearsals
  - Chat with actors about who they would prefer to have in the room using open questions
  - Actors review the Boundary Practice
  - Intimacy is staged using desexualized language of Ingredients. Don't step in.

STAGING SEX: A–Z **113**

- ◦ All kisses are worked using a placeholder with conversations and counts, objectives, etc.

- ◦ Stage management team and actors record choreography using desexualized language

- ◦ Stage management team also creates an audio recording of the choreography being dictated in time with actor lines

- During the Nudity Window

  - ◦ Robes are available for actors

  - ◦ No cell phones are allowed in the rehearsal room

  - ◦ All windows are covered

  - ◦ Back-up Plan is blocked

- Nudity and Intimacy during Tech

  - ◦ Nude actor is given sweatpants and a tee shirt that match their skin tone for nude scene while lights are being focused

  - ◦ Actors use Placeholders for kisses while cues are being written

  - ◦ Nudity Back-up Plan is teched

- When the Audience Arrives:

  - ◦ Content warnings are posted on the company website and outside of the theatre

  - ◦ Audience members are reminded to turn off their phones and that ushers will remove patrons with phones out during the performance

- Post Show

  - ◦ Actors De-Role

- At the Talkback

  - ◦ Share some information about the intimacy process

  - ◦ Continue to distinguish between the actors and the characters they play

- Post-Show Review

  - ◦ Ask questions about the process

  - ◦ Recognize successes

  - ◦ Work towards implementing necessary changes

STRATEGIES FOR ACTORS

All of the tools and techniques in this book can inform an actor's process. Here is a list of some of the most relevant:

- Ask questions.
    - Ask questions using the language of the Ingredients.
        - Who closes distance?
        - How long should the kiss last?
        - Who has the power in this moment?
    - Ask about when the intimacy is getting staged and who is staging it.
- Use the Boundary tools.
    - Talk about Buttons, Fences, and Gates with your scene partners.
    - Take them through the Boundary Practice with you.
        - Can I show you everywhere I'm giving you permission to touch me?
        - Can I take your hands? Say Button if you want to pause for a second.
        - Where did you see that you weren't supposed to touch me?
        - Now can you show me everywhere you're giving me permission to touch you?

STAGING SEX: A–Z   **115**

- Team up when there are problems.
  - Talk with your scene partner or another cast member.
  - Talk with your stage manager. Ask about a Chain of Communication.
  - If you don't have one, see if you can elect a Cast Deputy.
- Use Placeholders.
- Use Desexualized Language.
- Document the choreography and give it to the stage manager.
- De-role.

STRATEGIES FOR TEACHERS

Here are a few ideas to get you started bringing this work into your classroom, studio, or department:

- Teach the students to ask before they touch each other. Ask before you make any instructional touch.
- Model all of the big ideas (Consent, Desexualization, and Choreography) whenever you can.
- Teach the Boundary Practice.
  - Button
  - Fences
  - Gates
  - Boundary Practice Modification
  - Group Boundary Practice
- Teach Placeholder.
- Talk them through De-roling.
- Create a version of the Audition Disclosure Form and use it for scene assignments.
- Have students document where they rehearsed, who they were with, and what they accomplished. The documentation is important not only for them to be able to track their progress and for you to be able to follow along in their process, but also so that if there is a disagreement between students or an allegation of improper conduct, you have a written record of their work together.

116 STAGING SEX: A–Z

- Use Audition Disclosure Forms for department productions.

- Create a Chain of Communication and post it prominently.

If you are working with minors, be sure to check local laws regarding child labor and involve the parents or guardians heavily throughout the process. Consult with experts in your area before staging any intimacy with minors.

THE CHEAT SHEET

Implementing this full range of best practices, no matter your role, takes time and practice, and in the end, not every tool is for every artist. That's okay. Insisting that this work be implemented in its entirety for every artist would be counterproductive. Even a little bit better is better. This system is a toolkit designed to be applied as appropriate.

Identify the low hanging fruit where you can do better in your process and add things gradually. Everyone in a rehearsal process can identify one thing in each of the three big areas (establish a culture of consent, desexualize the process, and choreograph it) to work on. To make it easier to start, here are some simple things that you may be able to implement right away.

- Write casting breakdowns with clear descriptions of the requirements of a role.

- Use Audition Disclosure in casting.

- Distribute a Chain of Communication document with resources.

- Put intimacy, nudity, and sexual violence on the rehearsal schedule.

- Make "Ask before you touch" a company rule. Put it in company rules between "be on time" and "don't touch props that aren't yours."

- Introduce Button, Placeholder, and ask open questions.

- Use Boundary Practices.

- Check-in on boundaries once a week by giving the ensemble five minutes to review with their partners.

- Stop stepping in.

Desexualize the Process

- Use desexualized names for scenes.

- Use the language of the Ingredients.

- Stop making sex-related jokes and comments.

Documentation

- Draft a policy for directors about how your group is going to create a consent based process for staging intimacy, nudity, and sexual violence.

- Write choreography down using a common language (the Ingredients).
- If you are in academia or at a studio, require actors to document their out-of-class rehearsals.

Ten Ingredients

1. Opening and Closing Distance
2. Levels of Touch
3. Tempo and Counts
4. Shapes
5. Destination
6. Eye Contact
7. Visible Power Shifts
8. Breath and Sound
9. Gravity and Weight
10. Kissing

Remember: Even a little bit better is better. You can do this.

APPENDIX

Theatrical Intimacy Education

Theatrical Intimacy Education (TIE) is a consulting group and educational organization specializing in researching, developing, and teaching best practices for staging theatrical intimacy. Through training, TIE empowers artists with the tools to ethically, efficiently, and effectively stage intimacy, nudity, and sexual violence for theatre and film. TIE offers workshops, choreography services, residencies, consultations, and policy development support to professional and academic theatres and film companies across the United States.

TIE is led by co-founders Chelsea Pace and Laura Rikard. For more information about TIE and the growing faculty, visit www.theatricalintimacyed.com.

INDEX

"Abilene Paradox" 8
Angles 48, 49, 56, 66
apologies 38
Arcs 48–49, 56, 66, 87, 90–91, 93
arousal 9
audiences 84, 108, 109, 113
audio recordings 70, 113
Audition Disclosures 102–104, 112, 115, 116
auditions 104, 111–112

backup plans 83–84, 113
blocking 3, 81, 82
bone level of touch 42, 44–45, 46, 66, 90
boundaries 1, 4, 6; with audiences 109; Audition
    Disclosures 104; Boundary Practice exercise 17, 22,
    24–31, 68, 109, 112, 115, 116; Button 17–21; check-
    ins 15, 30, 116; consent 10; content warnings
    108; crossing 7, 12, 35–36, 37–38, 105; de-roling
    33–34; Destinations 50–51; Fences 21–23; Gates 23;
    mistakes 37–38; open questions 16; professional
    16, 36–37; recasting 105; Recipes 85; respecting 35;
    setting 9, 15; strategies for actors 114; Visible Power
    Shifts 54–55; vulnerability exercises 80
breaks 81, 82
Breath and Sound 57–58, 66, 68; embraces 86, 87;
    kissing 87; masturbation/digital stimulation 92–
    93; oral sex 90–91; penetrative sex 93; removing
    clothes 97
Button 17–21, 51, 116; Boundary Practice exercise 24,
    25, 27; first rehearsal 112; fittings 107; Recipes
    85; sexual violence 80–81; strategies for actors
    114; strategies for teachers 115; vulnerability
    exercises 80

casting 101, 102–105, 112, 116
cell phones 83, 108, 113
Chain of Communication 101–102, 112, 116
character descriptions 102, 111, 116
check-ins 15, 30, 81, 116
chemistry 5–6, 73
choreography 4–5, 7, 11–12, 13, 34, 39, 116;
    documentation 115; first rehearsal 112;
    Ingredients 65–66, 117; intimacy 9, 105–106,
    108; Levels of Touch 45–46; notating and
    coaching 68–70; rehearsals 112–113; sexual
    violence 81; strategies for teachers 115

Circle Game 20–21
Clay level of touch 42, 44, 46
clothes, removing 97
Communication, Chain of 101–102, 112, 116
company policies 101, 108, 109, 112, 116
conformity 8, 9
consent 9–10, 13, 15, 109, 112, 115, 116
content warnings 108, 111, 113
costume department 82–83, 95, 107
Counts 46–47, 68–69, 70, 96–97; Breath and Sound
    57; embraces 85–87; feeling and touching 95,
    96; kissing 61, 87–89; masturbation/digital
    stimulation 92–93; oral sex 90–91; penetrative
    sex 93; removing clothes 97; teasing 96, 97;
    Visible Power Shifts 56

dance choreography 4, 34
de-roling 33–34, 80–81, 82, 106, 113, 115
department policies 101
desexualization 10–11, 13, 35, 36, 39, 116;
    choreography 66, 70, 113; first rehearsal 112;
    Levels of Touch 42; production staff 106, 107;
    Recipes 85; sexual violence 80, 81; strategies for
    actors 115; strategies for teachers 115
designers 106, 107–108
Destinations 49–51, 52, 62, 68–69, 95, 96, 97
digital stimulation 50, 91–93, 98, 108
directors 3–4, 9; Chain of Communication 101; power
    dynamics 7–8, 9–10; professional boundaries
    36–37; stepping in 34–35
disabled artists 84
distance 40–41, 48–49; Breath and Sound 58;
    choreography 66; Counts 46, 47; embraces 85–87;
    Eye Contact 52; feeling and touching 95; Gravity
    and Weight 59; kissing 61, 63–64, 87–89; Levels of
    Touch 45, 46; masturbation/digital stimulation 92–
    93; oral sex 90–91; penetrative sex 93–95; sexual
    violence 81; strategies for actors 114; stylization
    98; teasing 97; vulnerability exercises 80
documentation 67, 70, 101, 115, 116–117
dress rehearsals 70

embraces 85–87; *see also* hugs
emotional safety 5
emotional support 16–17
emotions 6, 19

121

122 INDEX

energy 78
environmental factors 15–17
Eye Contact 51–52, 56, 64, 66, 68; embraces
85–87; feeling and touching 95; kissing 87–89;
masturbation/digital stimulation 92; oral sex
90–91; penetrative sex 93; removing clothes
97; sexual violence 81; teasing 96; vulnerability
exercises 78, 80

faces 22
feeling and touching 95–96, 98
Fences 21–23; Boundary Practice exercise 25, 28–29,
30, 68; feeling and touching 96; strategies for
actors 114; strategies for teachers 115
fight choreography 4–5, 34
Figure Eights 48, 49, 66, 93, 96
fittings 107
front of house staff 108

Gates 23, 114, 115
Gravity and Weight 58–60, 68; embraces 86; kissing
87; masturbation/digital stimulation 92; oral
sex 90; penetrative sex 93; removing clothes 97;
teasing 97
group Boundary Practice 29–30

hands 24–25, 41, 62, 63
handshakes 10–11
high-fives *see* Placeholders
hugs 16, 23; *see also* embraces

improvisation 65, 66, 68
Ingredients 39–84, 117; Breath and Sound 57–58;
choreography 65–66; Destinations 49–51;
documenting 67; Eye Contact 51–52; Gravity and
Weight 58–60; kissing 60–64; Levels of Touch
42–46; Opening and Closing Distance 40–41;
Recipes 67–71, 85; sexual violence 81; Shapes
47–49; Tempo and Counts 46–47; tweaking
66–67; Visible Power Shifts 52–57
intimacy calls 105
intimacy choreographers 9, 105–106, 108

jokes 36

kissing 60–64, 68; Audition Disclosures 102; on
bodies 98; choreography 11–12; Counts 46,
47; Destinations 49, 50; masturbation/digital
stimulation 92–93; old approaches to 2, 7;
penetrative sex 93–95; Placeholders 113; Recipe
87–89; strategies for actors 114

language 10–11, 12, 35; choreography 66, 70, 113;
first rehearsal 112; production staff 106; sex
positions 54, 55; sexual violence 80, 81; strategies
for actors 115

Levels of Touch 42–46, 68; choreography 66;
embraces 85–87; feeling and touching 95;
kissing 62, 63–64, 87–89; masturbation/digital
stimulation 92–93; oral sex 90–91; penetrative
sex 93–95; removing clothes 97; *see also* touch
light designers 107

marginalized groups 84
masturbation 91–93, 98
mental health 16
minors 116
mistakes 37–38
Moving 42, 43
Moving Together exercise 78–80
muscle level of touch 42, 43, 44–45, 46; Breath and
Sound 58; choreography 66; Counts 47; embraces
86, 87; kissing 63, 88, 89; masturbation/digital
stimulation 93; oral sex 90; penetrative sex 95;
Shapes 48

"no", saying 7–8, 10, 20
nudity 36, 82–84, 113; agreeing to 8; Audition
Disclosures 103; casting 102; company policies
101, 112; content warnings 108; post-show
reviews 109; rehearsal schedules 105, 116

"open", being 73–74, 75, 78
open questions 16, 61, 112, 116
Opening and Closing Distance 40–41, 48–49; Breath
and Sound 58; choreography 66; Counts 46, 47;
embraces 85–87; Eye Contact 52; feeling and
touching 95; Gravity and Weight 59; kissing
61, 63–64, 87–89; Levels of Touch 45, 46;
masturbation/digital stimulation 92–93; oral sex
90–91; penetrative sex 93–95; sexual violence 81;
strategies for actors 114; stylization 98; teasing
97; vulnerability exercises 80
oral sex 2, 89–91, 98, 108

Paint level of touch 42, 43, 44
Partner Up exercise 75, 77
passion 12
penetrative sex 93–95
personal relationships 37
photos 83
Placeholders 31–33, 62, 104, 112, 113, 115, 116
policies 101, 108, 109, 112, 116
post-show reviews 109, 113
Powder level of touch 42, 43, 46, 47
power dynamics 6, 7–8, 9–10; kissing 2; sexual
violence 81; stepping in 34–35; strategies for
actors 114; students 102; *see also* Visible Power
Shifts
production logistics 101–109
production managers 106, 108
production photos 83

production staff 106
professional relationships 37
projection designers 108
props 108
protocol 8–9, 12
Pulling 42–43, 44
Put It in Motion exercise 75–77

queer intimacy 84

recasting 104–105
Recipes 67–71, 85–99
rehearsals: Button 19; choreography 112–113;
    company policies 101; desexualization 11; nudity
    82, 83; Recipes 68; rehearsal time 13; schedules
    105, 112, 116; support during 16
reimagining 104–105
removing clothes 97
respect 8
reviews 109, 113
rhythm 46

self-care 80
sex positions 2, 54–55
sexual intercourse 93–95, 98, 108
sexual violence 5, 6, 80–82, 84; Audition Disclosures
    103; casting 102; company policies 101, 112;
    content warnings 108; post-show reviews 109;
    rehearsal schedules 105, 116
"sexy trap" 58
Shapes 41, 47–49, 56, 68; embraces 86; feeling and
    touching 95; kissing 64, 87, 89; masturbation/
    digital stimulation 92–93; oral sex 90–91;
    penetrative sex 93–95; removing clothes 97
sharing circles 5
"showmance" 6, 34
Simon Says 19–20
skin level of touch 42, 43, 44–45; choreography
    66; Counts 47; embraces 87; kissing 63, 88;
    masturbation/digital stimulation 93; oral sex 90;
    teasing 96
Social-Time boundaries 37
solidarity 36
Sound 57–58, 68; embraces 86; kissing 87;
    masturbation/digital stimulation 92–93; oral sex
    90–91; removing clothes 97

staffing 106
stepping in 34–35
stories 41
strategies for actors 114–115
strategies for teachers 115–116
stylization 98–99
survival instinct 74, 75
symbolic touch 98

talkbacks 109, 113
teachers 9, 115–116
team culture 9
teasing 96–97
technicians 106, 107–108
Tempo 46–47, 93–95
text 98
touch: boundary check-ins 15; Boundary Practice
    exercise 17, 24–31; company policies 101;
    embraces 85–87; feeling and touching 95–96;
    Fences 22–23, 25, 28–29, 30; Gates 23; oral sex
    90–91; strategies for teachers 115; stylization 98;
    vulnerability 77–78, 80; *see also* Levels of Touch
trauma 5, 6, 16, 34, 80–81
tweaking 66–67

verbal boundaries 21–23
violence 5, 6, 80–82, 84; Audition Disclosures 103;
    casting 102; company policies 101, 112; content
    warnings 108; de-roling 34; post-show reviews
    109; rehearsal schedules 105, 116
Visible Power Shifts 52–57, 59, 68, 98; embraces 86,
    87; feeling and touching 95; kissing 63, 64, 87,
    89; masturbation/digital stimulation 92; oral sex
    90; penetrative sex 93–95
vocabulary 12, 39, 54; *see also* language
vulnerability 6, 8, 73–80

Weight 58–60, 68; embraces 86; kissing 87, 89;
    masturbation/digital stimulation 92; oral sex 90;
    penetrative sex 93; removing clothes 97
What Ifs 56–57
Work-Time boundaries 37

"yes", saying 7–8, 10, 17, 20–21
young people 116